INTIMIDATION AND THE CONTROL OF CONFLICT IN NORTHERN IRELAND

IRISH STUDIES

IRISH STUDIES

Irish Studies presents a wide range of books interpreting important aspects of Irish life and culture to scholarly and general audiences. The richness and complexity of the Irish experience, past and present, deserves broad understanding and careful analysis. For this reason an important purpose of the series is to offer a forum to scholars interested in Ireland, its history, and culture. Irish literature is a special concern in the series, but works from the perspectives of the fine arts, history, and the social sciences are also welcome, as are studies which take multidisciplinary approaches.

Irish Studies is a continuing project of Syracuse University Press and is under the general editorship of Richard Fallis, associate professor of English at Syracuse University.

Irish Studies, edited by Richard Fallis

An Anglo-Irish Dialect Glossary for Joyce's Works. Richard Wall
Children's Lore in Finnegans Wake. Grace Eckley
The Drama of J. M. Synge. Mary C. King
Finnegans Wake: A Plot Summary. John Gordon
Fionn mac Cumhaill: Celtic Myth in English Literature. James MacKillop
Great Hatred, Little Room: The Irish Historical Novel. James M. Cahalan
Hanna Sheehy-Skeffington: Irish Feminist. Leah Levenson and Jerry Natterstad
In Minor Keys: The Uncollected Short Stories of George Moore. Edited by David B. Eakin and Helmut E. Gerber
Intimidation and the Control of Conflict in Northern Ireland. John Darby
Ireland Sober, Ireland Free: Drink and Temperance in Nineteenth-Century Ireland. Elizabeth Malcolm
Irish Life and Traditions. Edited by Sharon Gmelch
The Irish Renaissance. Richard Fallis
The Literary Vision of Liam O'Flaherty. John N. Zneimer
Northern Ireland: The Background to the Conflict. Edited by John Darby
Old Days, Old Ways: An Illustrated Folk History of Ireland. Olive Sharkey
Peig: The Autobiography of Peig Sayers of the Great Blasket Island. Translated by Bryan MacMahon
Selected Plays of Padraic Colum. Edited by Sanford Sternlicht
Selected Short Stories of Padraic Colum. Edited by Sanford Sternlicht
Shadowy Heroes: Irish Literature of the 1890s. Wayne E. Hall
Tinkers and Travellers. Sharon Gmelch
Ulster's Uncertain Defenders: Protestant Political, Paramilitary and Community Groups and the Northern Ireland Conflict. Sarah Nelson
Yeats. Douglas Archibald
Yeats and the Beginning of the Irish Renaissance, second edition. Philip L. Marcus

INTIMIDATION AND THE CONTROL OF CONFLICT IN NORTHERN IRELAND

JOHN DARBY

SYRACUSE UNIVERSITY PRESS

Preface

ETHNIC conflicts are distinguished from international wars because the combatants permanently inhabit the same battlefield. It is not possible to terminate hostilities by withdrawal behind national frontiers. Even during tranquil periods their lives are often intermeshed with those of their enemies. As a consequence, inter-community conflict is often characterised by internecine viciousness rather than by the more impassive slaughter of wars.

For this reason community conflicts, unless arrested at an early stage, tend to develop along predictable lines: they expand to involve a greater number of activists disputing a greater number of issues; disagreement grows into antagonism; enemies become more efficiently organised under more implacable leaders; the restraints on decent behaviour are weakened. As Coleman put it, 'the harmful and dangerous elements drive out those which keep the conflict within bounds'.

Against this general pattern, consider the conflict in Northern Ireland. Its origins, depending on one's political perspective, have been traced to various points between the twelfth century and 1969. Since 1969 the conflict has been persistently violent. There has certainly been ample time for the dangerous elements to drive out the restraining ones.

During the early 1970s, many observers believed that the upsurge of violence could only lead to two outcomes: the belligerents would either be shocked into an internal accommodation, or propelled into genocidal slaughter. Neither occurred. More than a decade later a settlement seemed further away than ever, and the level of violence, though remarkably persistent, had not intensified.

On the contrary, there is evidence that violence between the communities has diminished rather than grown. The casualty rate, having reached a peak of 468 deaths in 1972, had dropped to sixty-four in 1984. The proportion of civilian, as opposed to admitted combatant, deaths had diminished at an even greater rate. Rioting and direct sectarian confrontation, common in 1970, had become rare.

So why has the crisis in Northern Ireland not been resolved, either by a compromise settlement or genocidal carnage?

The answer is simple. There has been no resolution because the violence has not been intolerable. By whatever calculus communities compute their interests, the price of compromise is still thought to be greater than the cost of violence.

This shifts the balance of questioning. As well as asking why the violence is so persistent, we should ask why it has not been more severe. Instead of asking why people have tolerated such sustained disruption of their lives, we need to understand how they have tolerated it.

The core of the book deals with three small communities in Northern Ireland. The experiences of the people who live in them are not typical. On the contrary they have experienced much higher levels of violence, and live closer to the conflict, than most people in the province. All three communities have suffered greatly from intimidation and the evictions which followed it. It was for this reason that they were chosen, for the book aims to examine the process of community conflict through its most violent expression, and the ability of its victims to deal with the aftermath. What actually happens in a community which is experiencing violent disruption? What happens after the worst violence has passed? What are the mechanisms and controls which enable a return to some sort of normality?

The emphasis throughout is on interactions and relationships at local level. Discussions of 'the Northern Irish conflict' often concentrate on its political and international dimensions at the expense of its operation on the ground. The intention here is to examine the relationships between local interactions and these broader dimensions.

It will be argued that Northern Ireland's conflict is remarkable for the limitations on its violence rather than for the violence itself; that long familiarity with inter-community conflict within the north of Ireland has led to the evolution of effective mechanisms to control it; that these mechanisms arise from the mundane and essentially local accommodations reached in their own localities by people whose hostility has been modified by their need to carry on living in the same 'narrow ground'; and that the efficiency and variety of these mechanisms hold the key to explaining why a conflict of such duration has not produced more serious levels of violence. They have amounted, so far, to a major and effective control against the conflict expanding into a genocidal war.

This book has been a long time in the making. The research has its origins in 1972 when the Northern Ireland Community Relations Commission, alarmed by the high level of intimidation and enforced migration in Belfast, commissioned a research investigation into its process and effects. This was carried out by Geoffrey Morris and myself. My first acknowledgment is to him and the people who assisted us.

The subsequent direction of the research, and especially the decision to return after ten years to communities examined in the early 1970s, was influenced by many people. Particular thanks are due to academic colleagues from my own and other universities: to John Hickey who helped to establish a sociological framework for the empirical data; to my colleagues at the Centre for the Study of Conflict, especially Tony Hepburn, Nicholas Dodge, Seamus Dunn, Michael Poole and Ed Cairns, whose comments on the problem of defining intimidation were particularly helpful; to Leo Kuper and John Whyte for interest and guidance.

The opportunity to present research-in-progress papers at the Centre d'Etudes Irlandaises at the Sorbonne, the UCLA Sociology department and the Institute of Irish Studies at Queen's University Belfast, as well as in my own university, was invaluable both for the comments they provoked and for those they did not.

My main thanks are to the people who live and work in the communities, and who invariably gave their time and insights for no other reason than generosity.

John Darby
Centre for the Study of Conflict
University of Ulster
1986

Contents

THE BACKGROUND
1. Conflict and Contradictions   1
2. Conflict, Intimidation and Interaction in Northern
   Ireland   8
3. The Communities   30

INTIMIDATION
4. The Problem of Definition   51
5. Intimidation in the Communities   58
6. Intimidation: The Analysis   82

THE EFFECTS OF VIOLENCE
7. Relationships in the Communities   99
8. Contact after Intimidation   139
9. The Strengthening of the Heartlands   148
10. The Controls on Conflict   167
    Bibliography and References   175
    Appendix   179
    Notes   184

1.

Conflict and Contradictions

To make a theory of a conflict is to determine its
principal contradictions. (Boserup 1972)

VISITORS to Northern Ireland are often surprised by its confusing mixture of day-to-day normality and general violence.
When internment was introduced in August 1971, for example,
hordes of reporters were diverted from the world's other trouble
spots to Belfast. They were driven from the airport through
sunny, peaceful countryside into a city busy with shoppers.
Around the hotels favoured by visiting journalists there were few
obvious signs of disruption or violence. Yet less than a mile
away, as they soon discovered, people were being killed and
injured and more than 2,000 families had been forced by intimidation to evacuate their homes during the month of August.

The peace and the violence were aspects of the same reality.
One was as characteristic of Northern Ireland as the other. The
co-existence of normality and abnormality in such a small space
is one of Northern Ireland's many contradictions, and is rooted
in the dynamics of conflict and in the relationship between
conflict and violence.

Conflict and Violence

There has been dispute since the last century about whether
social conflict should be regarded as a disruptive or natural
phenomenon. The former view saw conflict as 'a disjunctive
process' (Wilson and Kolb 1949) and 'characterised by a
suspension of communication between the opposing parties'
(Lundberg 1939, 275) — a process which threatened existing
structures and the smooth running of society. However,
sociologists like Simmel, Coser and others have argued that, not

only is it impossible to conceive of a group which lacked inherent conflicts, but these apparently negative factors are essential elements in encouraging group formation and cohesion; they bind members together, define group boundaries and give people control over their own activities. Nevertheless this more positive view of social conflict has some serious limitations:

> The recognition of regulated conflicts of this kind as a permanent feature of all social structures is now recognised in sociology. They do not, however, adequately explain socially disruptive conflicts.
> (Rex 1968, 39)

A central issue in the dispute has been whether particular conflicts can only be understood by examining the circumstances of each society, or whether they are part of a general phenomenon. Certainly the unpredictability of most conflict appears to spring from the peculiar dynamics of each individual conflict. Shibutani and Kwan have indicated a number of these factors — technological innovation, demographic changes, education, war — but the variety is infinite, as are the forms of their interrelation.

> Insofar as conflict is a joint transaction, the course of events can be understood only as a succession of reciprocating adjustments that the combatants make to one another. What each side does is a response to the actual or anticipated moves of its opponents; thus, the course of events is built up by social interaction.
> (Shibutani and Kwan 1971, 135)

The work of James Coleman illustrates the benefits of conducting a detailed empirical analysis within a dynamic framework. Starting from the basis that each social conflict sets in motion its own dynamics, Coleman suggested that the process was carried on by two main characteristics — by changes in the issues under dispute, and by changes in the social organisation of the combatants. Issues in conflicts tend to shift from specific to general disagreements, from disagreement to antagonism, and from the original disputes to new ones. Among the changes which take place are growing polarisation , the formation of partisan associations, the emergence of new and more extreme leaders, and a growing reliance on word-of-mouth means of communication rather than the formal media. In addition to these general tendencies, however, Coleman emphasised the critical importance of reciprocity and interaction in reinforcing or diverting conflict:

> They constitute the chains which carry controversy from beginning to end as long as they remain unbroken, but which also provide the means of softening the conflict if methods can be found to break them. It is important to note that these reciprocal relations, once set in motion by outside forces, become independent of them and continue on their own.
>
> (Coleman 1971, 256)

Coleman argued that, as conflict progresses, 'the harmful and dangerous elements drive out those which keep the conflict within bounds', creating a 'Gresham's law of conflict' (Coleman 1971, 256).

The question is, under what circumstances do some minority groups initiate a process towards apparently inevitable defeat, and why do some dominant groups, but not others, set out to eliminate a weaker enemy?

Two main factors have been suggested as likely to influence whether a conflict remains peaceful or becomes violent. One is the rigidity of the social structures within each combatant group and the level of integration within the general society. If the conflict takes place within an agreed consensual framework, the parties will be less likely to conduct it in a way which endangers their common bonds; indeed, such societies develop institutions and mechanisms to facilitate the resolution of differences. However, if the conflict reflects a fundamental lack of consensus, its spread will not be modified by a reluctance to offend common interests and values: it is therefore more likely to become violent.

The other factor which helps to determine the level of violence is the degree to which a conflict is carried on for selfish motives or for some common aspiration. In Coser's words: 'Conflicts in which the participants feel that they are merely the representatives of collectivities and groups, fighting not for self but for the ideals of the group they represent, are likely to be more radical and merciless than those that are fought for personal reasons' (1971, 119). The crusading element in the conflict allows the commission of acts in good conscience, thus helping to explain the surprise and shock frequently expressed by combatants at acts they had committed during conflict. Further, if the selfless violence on behalf of the group is rooted in an ideology — as in a holy war or a revolutionary struggle — restraints upon it will be even fewer, and a willingness to offer and accept supreme sacrifices much greater.

To these two factors might be added a third which is less easily defined but more closely related to the cultural and traditional characteristics which are peculiar to each conflict. Conflict may take the form of racial riots in American cities, passive resistance in India, assassinations in Algeria, self-immolation in Vietnam or genocide in Ruanda. Each of these expressions of grievance or aggression emerges partly from the historical antecedents of each conflict, and are as natural a response by participants in one conflict as they are alien in another. In each case, however, there is a tendency for the form of protest to recur in successive outbreaks. When agitation is resumed after a dormant period, it looks back to the previous periods of dissent for its models. The importance of this observation is that some expressions of conflict may inherently be more likely to lead to violence than others. The nature of the Algerian and Lebanese conflicts of the 1950s and 1970s, for example, made civil war a likely outcome, whereas the sort of passive resistance encouraged by Ghandi and Martin Luther King applied strong pressure for political settlement. These peculiarities affect the rate as well as the pattern of conflict. A struggle which has rapidly intensified on previous occasions is more likely to reproduce a similar accelerated process. In effect, the stages through which it progresses, having been 'learned' during earlier fights, become compressed like the bellows of a concertina, and are therefore more difficult to divert. Accelerated progress towards violence is also more likely if the conflicting groups have established their own structures and organisations for the conduct of a violent struggle. These are more easily mobilised or diverted towards a more total form of warfare, and their very existence may contribute to such a development.

As Simmel has pointed out, however, few conflicts, from personal relationships to international wars, do not exhibit some restraints on behaviour:

> If a fight simply aims at annihilation, it does approach the marginal case of assassination in which the admixture of

unifying elements is almost zero. If, however, there is any consideration, any limit to violence, there already exists a socialising factor, even though only as a qualification of violence. (see Lawrence 1976, 140)

Indeed conflict tends to produce regulations and restraints upon the way it is conducted. It is not carried out in a vacuum, but in what Coser called 'a universe of binding norms' (1956, 124). Not only does it operate within such norms but, because the relationships between combatants inevitably alter during a conflict, it also encourages the adoption of new restraints to deal with the new conditions. The evolution of such controls is a consequence of the search by both sides for conventions which will limit the tendency for violence to become unrestrained, and which will therefore enable them to calculate the consequences of their violence. It is an application to conflict of the principle of limited liability.

An appreciation by combatants that their conflict is limited will certainly affect their conduct of it. The realisation that one's enemy is not bent on annihilation may encourage a search for compromise. It is also true that the same appreciation may actually encourage an increase in violence, in the belief that a weak opponent will be reluctant to follow along a similar route. In both cases the direction will be determined by the dynamics of the conflict, dynamics which are peculiar to the society in which it is being conducted.

The Northern Ireland Experience

The academic disputes about the role of conflict in society are echoed in the literature on the province's 'Troubles'. In general the predominant themes emphasised by historians and political scientists are dissention, violence and dysfunction. 'To the Irish all History is Applied History', according to Stewart, 'and the past is simply a convenient quarry which provides ammunition to use against enemies in the present' (Stewart 1977, 16). McCracken claimed that 'there is no floating vote on the constitutional issue' and Mansergh argued further that the resulting stalemate 'subordinates every vital issue, whether of social or economic policy, to the dead hand of sectarian strife' (Mansergh 1936). This general position was expressed in its most trenchant and pessimistic form by Rose:

Many talk about a solution to Ulster's political problem but few are prepared to say what the problem is. The reason is simple. The problem is that there is no solution.

(Rose 1976, 139)

A rather different picture is presented to those whose sole knowledge of Northern Ireland's conflict comes from reading community studies. Here the emphasis is on the relatively low influence of the conflict on day-to-day living. Certainly the conflict was acknowledged. Harris, for example, pointed out that 'all social relationships are pervaded by a consciousness of the religious dichotomy' (Harris 1971, xi). In most community studies, however, the emphasis is on the 'apparent harmony in local relations' (Donnan and McFarlane 1983, 135). Leyton argued that the values and structures shared by the occupants of the Catholic and Protestant villages which he studied had led to long and healthy stability. 'This recognition of the humanity of the other side — "We're all the one blood if you go back far enough" — is apparent even in times of extreme political tension' (Leyton 1974, 194). Despite the central conflict, as Heslinga put it, the people of the north shared 'a sense of regional fellowship, a sense of difference from southerners, that mixture of contempt and defensiveness that is typical of the strongly-marked provincial character' (Heslinga 1962, 102).

The scene described is fashioned by the interests of the observer and by the academic prism through which it is viewed.

Most of the studies which describe ordinary people going about their activities untouched by the conflict were carried out in rural areas or small towns. Burton's study of Anro, a Catholic community in Belfast, is the only one rooted in an urban setting in the heart of the Troubles. Arguing that the press cannot penetrate how the Catholics living in Anro constructed the meaning of events, he claimed that their social consciousness was formed from three interconnected elements: the importance of community, the consciousness and institutionalisation of sectarian identity, and republicanism in its broad, cultural sense rather than a narrow political one. Together they give the community its 'gemeinschaft', which has expanded to take in the new relationships and priorities created by the war. It is a more uncompromising image of conflict than that observed in the more tranquil rural communities studied by Harris, Leyton, Blacking and Buckley.

Which picture is more accurate? The problem is that they do not describe the same image. Some communities are exclusively Protestant or Catholic, others mixed; some have been seriously scarred by violence, others unaffected; some are urban and others rural. The conditions are greatly varied. The research findings are not at variance at all, if their aim is only to describe a great variety of different settings, but some make larger claims. Burton's assertion that Anro is 'taken as typical of the community structure of the Northern Irish Catholic' (Burton 1978, 3), for example, is not easily sustained. The main message from the rich and varied evidence accumulated through local studies is that there is no typical community structure.

2.

Conflict, Intimidation and Interaction in Northern Ireland

Intimidation: The historical background

The Pound district has for many years been chiefly inhabited by a Roman Catholic population, while Sandy-row district has been chiefly inhabited by a population of Orangemen and Protestants. Until lately, however, there was some inter-mixture, a few Catholics residing in the Sandy-row district, and a few Protestants in the Pound district. Since the commencement of the late riots, however, the districts have become exclusive, and by regular systematised movements on both sides, the few Catholic inhabitants of the Sandy-row district have been obliged to leave it, and the few Protestant inhabitants of the Pound district have been also obliged to leave that locality.

These removals were often kindly enough effected on both sides: friendly notices to quit were often given; and the extreme penalty for non-compliance — namely, the wrecking of the house — was, in many instances, not resorted to until the lapse of some time after such notice.

(Belfast Riot Inquiry 1857)

The riots mentioned in this extract have not taken place in this decade: they do not even belong to this century. However the commissioners who wrote the report on the Belfast riots of 1857 were describing an early example of enforced population movement resulting from intimidation, and their description featured many forms of violence which frequently recurred — the eviction of minorities, increased polarisation and the wrecking of homes.

The origins of this conflict considerably pre-date the riots of 1857. The conquest of Ulster, and the subsequent colonisation of parts of the province during the early seventeenth century, produced a demographic pattern where the native Irish were concentrated in different areas from those of the colonising Scots and English (see for example Beckett 1952 and 1956 and Lyons 1971). The newcomers differed significantly from the native Irish in religion, language, social customs and economic status.

Nevertheless, despite attempts to maintain distinctions between the two communities, there was considerable mixing from the start; Buchanan has described the cultural overlap between the Irish and the Planters, especially those from Scotland (Buchanan 1982), and the attempts to retain demographic segregation were informally abandoned soon after the Plantation. From the start the differences between the dominant Planters and the subordinate Gaels were occasionally expressed in violent terms.

Until the early nineteenth century the violence was essentially rural and was expressed through informal and illegal associations. In most parts of Ireland it was directed against the state and its institutions. As Townshend has demonstrated, collective rural violence was a bewildering confusion of faction fighting, grievances about land, political protest and 'elements of carnival'. Popular reactions to it were often ambivalent. Many disapproved of its forms, but few did not have some sympathy with its causes:

> The better farmers are more anxious to have these parties [the Ribbonmen] put down, yet they would sooner surrender their arms and property than give any information to the authorities.   (Townshend 1983, 18)

In Ulster, where the balance between Protestants and Catholics was closer than in other parts of Ireland, rural violence was also fuelled by sectarian rivalry. 'The sectarian divide was too functional to be permitted to disappear' (Townshend 1983, 46). Changes in land ownership and tenancies were the measure of success or failure, and were tenaciously resisted or sought. While the intensity of sectarian violence fluctuated greatly, it was a nagging backcloth to the day-to-day living of many communities in nineteenth-century Ulster.

With the growth of industrial Belfast from the early nineteenth century, sectarian violence became increasingly an urban phenomenon. Between 1835 and 1935 there were eight periods of serious rioting in Belfast — in 1835, 1857, 1864, 1872, 1886, 1898, 1920-22 and 1935 — and many years during which some disturbances have been recorded (see Boyd 1969 and Budge and O'Leary 1973). There were also two serious riots in Londonderry — in 1869 and 1884. Five of these were sufficiently alarming to produce official inquiries, and their findings provide a record of urban tensions. Apart from the reports themselves, the verbal and written evidence which accompanied them gives insights into relationships between the two communities. They also permit longitudinal comparisons with similar reports from the riots of 1969-71, especially the Cameron and Scarman reports, and with data collected during this research. There were disadvantages, however, in that witnesses could not be compelled to attend, cross-examination was strictly controlled and, except in the later reports, witnesses were not sworn. The other main sources of information were contemporary reports by citizens, newspapers and visitors to the city; in some cases, these can be used to verify the evidence of witnesses.

One of the early riots in Belfast was in fact recorded by an English visitor in 1835, twenty-two years before the first official report. John Barrow visited the city on 12 July, Orangeman's day, when disturbances broke out over an arch in Sandy Row, the Riot Act was read and a woman was shot. The novelty of the incident was remarked by Barrow:

> Though riots of this kind are not of unusual occurrence in the great towns of Ireland, and happen but too frequently in some of those of Great Britain; yet here, in Belfast, where every one is too much engaged in his own business, and where neither religion nor politics have interfered to disturb the harmony of society, it could not fail to create a great and uneasy sensation.   (Barrow 1835, 35-36)

While there would be little profit in describing the riots which dotted the subsequent century and a half in Ulster, some aspects of the origins, developments and forms have particular relevance to the theme of intimidation.

Despite considerable variation in the intensity and duration of the riots, the occasions which led to them were remarkably similar. There was a sharp increase in the Roman Catholic populations of both Belfast and Londonderry during the early eighteenth century. Barrow described how 'some four or five thousand raw, uneducated Catholic labourers from the south had, within a few years, poured into the city, to supply the demand for labour' (Barrow 1835, 33). In Londonderry too, as the 1869 commissioners remarked, 'trade and commerce attracted population, much of it from the Roman Catholic county of Donegal' (Londonderry Riots Inquiry 1889, 15). In both cities the religious communities were concentrated in particular and adjoining districts. This provided the backcloth to the urban riots.

There is no discernible relationship between economic conditions and the tendency towards rioting. Violence broke out during periods of prosperity and depression. However almost all the major riots emerged from a combination of general political unrest and a particular catalytic incident. The former occasions included the 1886 and 1893 Home Rule bills, political meetings (Londonderry 1869 and 1884), the centenary celebrations for the 1798 rebellion and the introduction of partition (1920-22). The catalysts varied greatly in form: the funeral of an early victim, an argument between two navvies in the shipyard which led to a drowning, the pulling down of an Orange arch etc. Rioting was predominantly a summer activity, and the annual marches and celebrations which marked July and August were often the immediate cause of fighting or led to its intensification. The Londonderry commissioners in 1869, referring to the annual demonstrations by the Protestant Apprentice Boys on 12 August, observed that in recent years 'the character of the demonstrations has certainly undergone a change, and, among the Catholic lower classes at least, they are now regarded with the most hostile feelings' (Londonderry Riot Inquiry 1869, 15). The Apprentice Boys were involved in both of the city's riots. In Belfast the 1857 riot commissioners singled out the Orange marches on 12 July as 'the originating cause of the riots' (Belfast Riot Inquiry 1857, 8); the point was made more graphically in the cross-examination of Francis Keenan, a Catholic worker in the Belfast shipyards, in 1887. Asked whether sectarian fighting was an unusual occurrence, he replied:

Oh, it is an annual occurrence. Every year it is just the same. They stick up everywhere all through the place, 'Away with the Fenians', and I saw posted on the boiler house, 'All Fenians clear out, by order of the RBC', which I take to mean the Rivet Boys' Club.   (Belfast Riot Inquiry 1887, 444)

As a consequence, one of the most frequent suggestions of witnesses appearing before the riot commissions was that the processions should be curtailed in some way.

A major preoccupation of all the reports was the conduct of police and magistrates, and consideration of how the riots might best be controlled — also a main concern for the Cameron report in 1969. One feature was common to all the disturbances: the inability of any form of police force to establish a neutral stance in Belfast's sectarian disputes. In 1857 the main responsibility for policing was in the hands of a local force of 160 men, controlled by Belfast Corporation. As the commissioners pointed out, 'the police force are, with six or seven exceptions, entirely Protestant, and those in any command amongst them are exclusively so; a great many of them are, or have been, Orangemen' (Belfast Riot Inquiry 1857, 4). Consequently they were severely attacked by Catholic rioters. By 1886, however, the Royal Irish Constabulary (RIC) had assumed the main responsibility for policing. Many of the policemen were marked as southerners by their accents and presumed to be Catholics. Protestant grievances about the anti-Protestant bias of the RIC were a main preoccupation of the witnesses in 1887. Consequently if one side regarded the police with hostility, the other side often regarded them as comrades. In the 1886 riots, for example, Protestant witnesses described how Catholic crowds applauded the RIC as they attacked Protestant crowds. In 1857 a Protestant local policeman, Mr Bindon, described the hostility when he arrested a Protestant: 'They thought I was a bad Protestant when I arrested some of their own party' (ibid, 56).

The term 'intimidation' was commonly used by witnesses during the 1864 inquiry, replacing the more sedate 'removal' of earlier accounts. There was little sign of misunderstanding about its function. From the 1857 inquiry, the process which witnesses described was clearly designed to rid alien elements from districts, factories and services:

The separation of these two districts (i.e. the Pound and Sandy Row) into exclusive encampments appears to us to be little more than the preparation for the festivals of July, and the clearing out of the supposed supporters of the opposite classes to prepare the respective districts for the scenes which follow the celebration of these festivals.   (ibid, 2)

In the earlier years, this 'separation' was often a relatively peaceful process, involving threats rather than violence. Ellen Grant, a Roman Catholic victim from Combermore Street, told the commissioners:

They said they would not disturb us at that hour of the morning [3 o'clock], but they would give us until six tomorrow evening to leave, for they had orders from the authorities of the town that none of our class should live in that locality.   (ibid, 138)

The Grants, and two neighbouring families, took what was described as the 'gentle hint'. One of the other two, Betty Donohue, was warned by a Presbyterian neighbour of a possible attack; when asked if this warning was kindly intended, she replied, 'Oh, indeed it was kindly intended, for my husband and him were very intimate' (ibid, 87). Sarah Anne Charlewood, a Protestant victim, was similarly warned by a Roman Catholic neighbour:

A woman come and told me to leave there that night, for she heard them say that if I was not out of there on Sunday night my corpse would leave on Monday morning.   (ibid, 198)

The most accessible enemy was the one living in one's midst — the Protestant who lived in a Catholic area, the Catholic who had married a Protestant. The first three victims of the 1857 riots, and probably the first recorded specific cases of intimidation in Belfast, were all mixed-religion families; in two cases the husbands were Catholic.

Although the extract from the 1857 report quoted at the start of this chapter referred to 'regular systematised movements on both sides', the evidence itself suggests that they were relatively spontaneous. In the later riots, however, the process of intimidation became more systematic. In 1886, for example, eleven Protestant families were ejected forcibly from Argyll Street (Belfast Riot Inquiry 1887, 688). The eviction of people from workplaces was also common, and the shipyards and docks were the centres of many attacks on Catholic workmen. During the same 1886 riots, public houses became major targets for the first time and at least forty were attacked and destroyed, thirty-eight of them owned by Catholics (ibid, 7 and 9). John Riordan, one of the publicans, considered that the reason for this new concentration was the fact that 320 of Belfast's 400 public houses were owned by Roman Catholics (ibid, 496).

A Catholic priest, Fr John Tohill, presented a list of Catholic businesses wrecked in Protestant districts, and suggested that the attacks were systematic: 'The conviction in the minds of the Catholics was that there was a determination to drive Catholics, because of their religion, out of Protestant districts' (ibid, 508). The subsequent expulsion of 700 Catholics from their work during the 1898 riots (Boyd 1969, 175), of 2,000 from the shipyards in 1912 (Gribben 1982, 49) and the activities of the Ulster Protestant League in 1935, appear to suggest that some of the enforced movements were caused by organised activities as well as by the immediate anger of individuals.

During the course of the riots there were strong pressures for people to conform to the standards and behaviour of their communities. Indeed it is clear from the evidence presented to the inquiries that there were strong sanctions against crossing to the other side. Members of the Orange Order during the 1850s had been expelled for marrying Catholics (Belfast Riot Inquiry 1857, 10). One Captain Venner, a magistrate, when cross-examined about discrimination on appointments to the magistrates' bench, suggested that the low number of Catholic magistrates was partly explained by their unwillingness to join the side of the authorities.

Mr Lynch: How many Catholics are there?
Captain Venner: There is only one gentleman that I know of — one who is a Roman Catholic. I believe he is the only one competent to fill the situation, and, at the same time, willing to accept of it.   (ibid, 219)

During periods of violence the pressures to conform with one's co-religionists were much greater. During the same inquiry, a

Mrs Donohue described an attack on a Protestant house by a Protestant mob. When asked to explain it she replied that it was 'because he would not join among the rest of them' (ibid, 89). Suspicion of collaboration indeed came high on the list of un-forgivable actions. Thus in 1886 one witness described the community's reaction to his giving evidence against rioters:

> I live in Newtownards Road; but, my Lord, 'Mike Hale, the informer' is even written up on the walls in the Ballymacarret direction. That is the thanks I got for trying to save the old man that is old enough to be my grandfather, and the police must know it.   (Belfast Riot Inquiry 1887, 385)

Group cohesion and conformity during a period of riot was sometimes a reaction against either a perceived or actual threat from the other side. Provocation was common. Hugh Hanna, a 'controversial preacher' whose open-air sermons at the Custom House were regarded as inflammatory by the 1857 commissioners, instructed his listeners, who were occupying a major thoroughfare: 'Where you assemble around, leave so much of the thoroughfare unoccupied that such as do not choose to listen may pass by. Call that clearance, "the pope's pad".' (Belfast Riot Inquiry 1857, 13). The immediate cause of the 1864 riots was a mock funeral of Daniel O'Connell, held on the Boyne Bridge seventeen years after his actual death, in clear sight of his Catholic supporters (Belfast Riot Inquiry 1864, 21). In addition to these specific actions, the annual celebrations and marches were also regarded as provocative. The Londonderry commissioners believed that the key to the city's sectarian strife was the existence of two groups in the standing relation to each other of a dominant and a subject caste, to whom the celebration of the city's defence in 1689 was 'the proudest recollection of one section' and 'bitter humiliation' for the other (Londonderry Riot Inquiry 1869, 15). The use of party songs was often remarked — 'The Wearing of the Green', 'Croppies lie down', 'Derry Walls' — but complicated by the common tendency of attaching party words to traditional or popular airs. As the Londonderry commissioners earnestly pointed out:

> A band accompanied the procession; but does not seem to have played any party-tunes. Here, indeed, we may interpose

the remark that it is difficult to say what is not a party-tune in
Derry; for the most innocent airs, if played by a particular
band, assume, at once, for another section of the people, a
party character.   (ibid, 17)

A necessary prerequisite for community conflict is the
generalisable characteristics of group membership. It is not
possible to discriminate in the appointment of policemen or
magistrates unless members of the disadvantaged group can be
recognised. Some members of the Belfast Police Committee,
which hired the local policemen in 1864, were confident of their
ability to do this. Isaac Murphy, for example, explained to the
inquiry that the committee 'appointed the biggest men — men
most likely able to knock other men down. Belfast is inhabited
by two races of people — the one the colonial or Scotch race, and
the other the natural Celtic race; and the Scotchmen are the
biggest' (Belfast Riot Inquiry 1864, 82). The superintendant of
the local police, when asked if he knew 'that Barney, Michael or
Patrick were almost always Catholic names', replied, 'I have
heard you say so' (ibid, 83). Samuel Black, Chairman of the
Policy Committee, was cross-examined by Commissioner
Dowse on the same issue:

Black: The great majority of the small farmers in that district
are Protestants and it is principally from their sons that the
appointments are to be made, inasmuch as they are the
strongest class of men, generally speaking.
Dowse: Do you mean physically?
Black: Yes, they are generally stronger than the lower classes
of the Roman Catholics: besides, I think they are better
educated.
Dowse: You look at the candidates before appointing them?
Black: In some cases I could tell a man's religion by his face,
but not always.   (ibid, 123)

This claim that it was possible to tell religion by names, size,
education or general appearance clearly intrigued the commissioners, who frequently asked other witnesses about it. Most
of these denied the ability. When another committee member,
Robert McGeach, was asked by Dowse if he could tell a man's
religion from his look, the reply was, 'Certainly not. When I

lived in Tyrone I thought I could, but I could not do it in Belfast' (ibid, 208). Nevertheless, there were no cases of mistaken identities recorded among the victims of attack during the riots.

There were a number of cases in all the riots between 1835 and 1935 which demonstrated that intimidation did not meet with the approval of all the members of intimidating groups. Instances were recorded of victims being rescued and protected, sometimes with unfortunate consequences for the protector. In 1886, for example, the Protestant neighbour who gave shelter to Patrick Cox when his shop was destroyed was subsequently boycotted and forced to sell his own business (Belfast Riot Inquiry 1886, 495). The clergy were often praised for their moderating influence and in 1912 patrolled the Pound district to prevent the celebrations for the reading of the Home Rule bill expanding into a riot (Gribbon 1982, 49). The 1864 commissioners were sufficiently moved by the evidence of a Presbyterian clergyman, the Rev. Isaac Nelson, to quote from it at length in their report:

> My Protestant neighbours remained up, wandering round the houses, playing 'The Protestant Boys' and 'The Boyne Water', and using phraseology which I hope will in future be foreign to the towns of this island. Having taken possession of the highway, they maltreated, in spite of all my remonstrances, every passer-by who would not use certain language. I am speaking of a number of persons with whom I have been to a certain extent acquainted for years, and can state to be most well conducted and quiet persons. I saw that crowd come up to the houses of four poor members of the Latin Church. I did not then know myself exactly their religious denomination. I saw the furniture broken to pieces on the floor, and I saw the houses, as you express it, gutted. . . . The mobs in my neighbourhood not only hunted poor Roman Catholic neighbours out of their houses, but I had to go and beseech them to grant so many hours to these poor people to take their furniture out of the place. I had also to go and get horses and carts to remove the furniture, and I had a great deal to do to repress the violence of the mob.

The forms of violence in Belfast were not fundamentally altered by partition, reflecting as they did more traditional and more local hostilities. The 1935 riots appear to have involved more direct provocation than their predecessors, but were otherwise rather similar (see Boyd 1969, 178). In 1964 a dispute over the exhibition and removal of a tricolour flag from the republican headquarters in Divis Street resembled the 1857 riots in their location and fighting between Catholics and the police. The 1969 riots too were marked by criticism of police behaviour, hostile crowds, processions and intimidation. They were fought out in the same streets as those of 1857.

Whose conflict?

The riot reports of the nineteenth and twentieth centuries chronicle a tradition of urban violence between Catholics and Protestants, but they also present a distorted picture. By definition their subject was exceptional. They were written about periods when public order had broken down and made few references to the other years when disruption was minimal. Further, they were concerned only with Belfast and Londonderry and, in the main, only with relatively small districts within the cities. While this research is also primarily concerned with communities affected by exceptional violence, it is important to provide a perspective by looking first at the literature on Protestant-Catholic relations in Northern Ireland.

The recent acceleration in publications about the Northern Irish conflict underlines the intimacy of the relationship between public interest and academic activity. In 1976 a bibliography of the Northern Irish conflict detailed more than 800 references, of which 580 had been published in the six years since the outbreak of violence in 1969 (Darby 1976). More recent bibliographies have demonstrated that the traffic has not diminished (Eager 1980; O'Dowd, Rolston *et al.* 1983).

The earlier lack of interest in the subject was not entirely due to the generally unfashionable nature of ethnic studies, nor to the generally mundane and non-confrontational relationships between Catholics and Protestants in Northern Ireland before 1969. It also arose from a gradual shift among historians and social scientists in their definitions of the boundaries and nature of the conflict and the combatants. The creation of the Northern Ireland unit in 1921 and the development of separate institutions north and south of the border made it increasingly difficult for historians to treat developments in the two parts of Ireland in an integrated manner. Social scientists also have become more inclined to treat Northern Ireland's community problems as peculiar. Rosemary Harris' study of Ballybeg in 1952-53 made it clear that the villagers there interacted within a fundamentally Northern Irish context. Barritt and Carter entitled their pioneering social survey *The Northern Ireland Problem* and presented a study of what was clearly an agreed, if divided, society. This view has been largely endorsed by subsequent writers.

This does not imply that both groups had a similar attitude towards the state. On the contrary, while the Northern Ireland state came to acquire a positive reality for its Protestant majority, for its Catholic minority the reality was a reactive one. Protestant nationalism, deeply suspicious of Britain, had become primarily attached to Northern Ireland; Catholics, on the other hand, continued to regard it with suspicion. However the passage of time had produced among many some measure of reluctant acceptance of the six-county unit, if only because alternative accommodations would present greater problems. Every poll and survey since the 1960s has shown a substantial level of Catholic support for a settlement within Northern Ireland, with certain conditions attached. In 1968, for example, Richard Rose found that thirty-three per cent of Catholics approved of Northern Ireland's constitutional position, and a further thirty-two per cent did not express an opinion; in another poll in 1972, forty-one per cent of Catholics said that they would vote against the unification of Ireland, and six per cent that they would abstain. Sixty years of existence have given Northern Ireland a level of *de facto* recognition, even from its opponents. In 1972 JC Beckett summed it up:

> A fifty-years experience has not given Northern Ireland either unity or stability: but it has defined the political, economic and social problems of the area in specifically local terms. Even if Northern Ireland, as a separate political unit, were to be abolished, it would, in a real sense, survive, and carry into the foreseeable future the characteristics that have developed from the settlement imposed in 1920.
>
> (Beckett 1972)

Within this unit, however, there has been wide agreement about the composition of the two groups engaged in the conflict. Long before Ireland was partitioned the English historian Moneypenny described these groups as two nations:

> The Home Rule struggle is a struggle between two nations, the Protestants and the Roman Catholics, or as, to avoid the semblance of ministering to religious bigotry, they had better be called, the Unionist and the nationalist.
>
> (Moneypenny 1912)

Seventy years later, and in a Northern Ireland setting, a substantial body of evidence indicates that Catholics and Protestants in the province perceived themselves as belonging to distinct groups, and perceived the conflict to be rooted in their differences. It also indicates that these perceptions are based on actual distinctions.

1. Perceived Differences

The consciousness of group differences is most tellingly illustrated by the novels, poetry and autobiographies of Ulster people. McCann, who grew up in the Catholic Bogside district of Derry, remarked: 'We were never taught to hate Protestants. Rather we were taught to accept that it was for the best that we did not know them. We resented them, of course, in a generalised way. We told one another to "just ignore them"' (McCann 1974, 21). Robert Harbinson, growing up in the Protestant Sandy Row district of Belfast, recounted the fear of Papal conspiracy, and describes his Orange Order excursion to Bangor, where 'from the safety of the passing train, we could boldly hurl abuse at the Mickeys' houses and their papish murals' (Harbinson 1960, 130). Linked to this antagonism was a firm conviction, infrequently tested, in the universal ability to recognise the other side. As John Hewitt put it, in a powerful poem comparing Northern Ireland's Protestants with the Romans during the declining days of empire:

> You may distinguish,
> if you were schooled with us by pigmentation,
> by cast of features or by turn of phrase,
> or by the clan-names of them which are they,

among the faces moving in the street.
They worship Heaven strangely, having rites
we snigger at, are known as superstitious,
cunning by nature, never to be trusted,
given to dancing and a kind of song
seductive to the ear, a whining sorrow.
Also they breed like flies.... (Hewitt 1950)

The academic literature confirms the strength of perceived differences. O'Donnell's examination of the attitudes held by Catholics and Protestants in Northern Ireland demonstrated a high level of stereotyping across the religious divide, so that 'both groups see themselves as decent, fine, ordinary people, but see each other as bitter or brainwashed' (O'Donnell 1977). As a consequence, considerable importance was attached to group cohesion; a survey in 1970, for example, concluded that fifty-eight per cent of both religious groups believed that co-religionists should 'stick together and do a lot to help each other' (ITA 1970). It was the opinion of Jackson and others that the strong group identification arose from mutual fear:

> So this is the first point to make: That virtually everyone in Northern Ireland feels himself under threat and reacts accordingly. There is no inclination for reason or compromise simply because the most urgent need is to combat a threat which may seem small or non-existent to outsiders, but looms obliteringly over those locked into the situation.
>
> (Jackson 1971, 6)

The sense of threat was heightened during periods of intense violence, and appeared to be stronger outside the most segregated heartlands than inside them. During the Belfast riots of the late 1960s, for example, the incidence of suicide and nervous disorders remained low in the riot areas, but increased sharply in neighbouring peaceful districts (Lyons 1976, 50). Another study of those families which had been intimidated from their homes between 1969 and 1973 confirmed that their preferred choice for a new house was within the most segregated parts of the city, where they could feel more secure (Darby and Morris 1974).

Despite the common hostility and apprehension, it is clear

that there are significant differences in mutual group perceptions, although not all researchers have agreed on the nature of the differences: 'Catholics see discord in nationality terms whereas Protestants see it in religious terms', Rose claimed; 'Politics in Northern Ireland involves ideologically unrelated conflicts' (Rose 1971, 216). Heskin supported this view, and went on to suggest that, 'whereas Protestants objected primarily to Catholics as representatives of a religious group, Catholics objected primarily to Protestants as people' (Heskin 1980, 47). Jackson, on the other hand, believed that Protestant stereotypes of Catholics — as feckless, dirty and sexually unrestrained — were essentially racial, and almost indistinguishable from English views of racial immigrants or Israeli views of Arabs. He went on to make the point that general stereotypes of the out-group were not applied in practice to its individual members:

> At individual level one never finds that these faults are singled out. No matter how viciously a man may attack the other religion as a group, he will always make an exception of the members he knows personally.   (Jackson 1971, 9)

Both these suggestions — that cross-cultural stereotypes differed for the two groups, and that there was little relationship between stereotyping and actual cross-cultural contact — find support in recent research into segregated schooling. Despite acknowledged ignorance about each other's schools, teachers in Catholic and Protestant schools had strong and discernably different perceptions of each other:

> The most common characteristic attributed to Roman Catholic schools by Protestant teachers was the role of the church in the school's affairs; on the other hand, the description of Protestant schools by Catholic teachers frequently included such terms as 'cold', 'rigid' and 'more academic'. These descriptions were used with great consistency.
> (Darby *et al.* 1977, 67)

2.   Real Differences

The distinctions between the two religious groups did not exist merely in their perceptions of each other. There were also real differences in terms of economic prosperity, demographic location, institutional arrangements and social relationships.

Birrell has demonstrated, in a useful synthesis of research on the subject, that Catholics not only perceived themselves to be economically deprived in relation to Protestants, but that their perception was well founded (Birrell 1972): they were more likely to be unemployed, to be paid lower wages and to live in inferior housing. Like many others, he suggested that there was a direct relationship between deprivation and minority discontent (see de Paor 1970; Boserup 1972).

The demographic location of the two groups, in broad terms, also marked a difference between them. Generally, Protestants predominated in the eastern counties of Antrim and Down and in Belfast, while Catholic majorities were more common in the areas closest to the border with the Irish Republic. In some areas, notably the working-class districts of Belfast and Londonderry, polarisation was high. Even before the current violence started, two-thirds of Belfast's families lived in streets in which more than ninety per cent of the households professed the same religion (Poole and Boal 1973, 14).

There were also institutional links which bound together each community and excluded the other. Political allegiance and religious adherence were highly correlated, and various attempts to establish bi-confessional political parties — notably the Northern Ireland Labour Party during the 1950s and 1960s, and the Alliance Party since 1971 — have only confirmed that the political middle group does not attract the support of more than ten-fifteen per cent of the population. As the historian McCracken expressed it, 'there is no floating vote on the constitutional issue' (McCracken 1967). Schools were also highly segregated by religion, especially at primary level. In 1976, more than seventy per cent of schools participating in a survey had no children from the religious minority group; a further twenty-six per cent had religious minorities of less than five per cent. Among teachers the level of polarisation was even higher: only 1.5 per cent of the teachers in the survey taught in schools where the predominant religion was different from their own (Darby *et al* 1977, 25-28).

Social interaction between the two groups reflected these differences. 'In general the social network of the individual is based

overwhelmingly in most fields on ties with his co-religionists',
wrote Rosemary Harris; 'All social relationships are pervaded
by a consciousness of the religious dichotomy' (Harris 1972, x).
The dominance of the central schism has been a major theme in
many other studies (Barritt and Carter 1962, Rose 1971, Leyton
1974). More detailed studies of a Protestant community in
Belfast (Nelson 1982) and of a Roman Catholic community in
the same city (Burton 1980) confirmed the denominational
exclusiveness of some working class urban districts, and supplemented the research by Harris and Leyton in rural areas of
counties Tyrone and Down.

Within these polarised districts both groups exhibited a high
level of self-sufficiency. Boal examined a wide range of social
relationships between two highly segregated urban districts,
including school attendance, shopping patterns, social visiting
and newspaper readership: he concluded that 'the cumulative
evidence indicates the presence of two very distinct territories'
(Boal 1971, 8). Harris, describing shopping patterns in the small
village of Ballybeg, also confirmed that 'the advantages offered
by one shop over its rivals had to be very considerable before a
Protestant owner could attract Catholic customers, and vice
versa' (Harris 1972, 6).

Leisure activities were also highly segregated in Ballybeg,
partly because dances, film shows and sports were often
organised by the churches. When cross-religion contact
occurred, it was mainly in middle-class settings like golf or tennis
clubs, or at formal dances at the local hospital — an observation
supported by Kirk's study of Lurgan, a town in County
Armagh. Kirk found similar middle-class mixing, but a high
level of separate and parallel leisure provision among workers: a
Protestant Mechanics' Institute and a Catholic Working Men's
Club; the Irish National Foresters (Catholic) and the Masons
(Protestant); two religiously segregated old people's homes.

Such a high level of segregation between the two groups
depended, to some extent on a system of recognition, or 'telling',
as Burton called it, by which the group membership of strangers
could be assessed. Cairns and others have pointed out that this
discrimination is based 'not upon perceptual cues but upon
stereotyped cues' (Cairns 1980, 117); consequently, without
obvious indicators like skin colour, the cues were more difficult

to acquire. According to Cairns, the most frequently used cues were, in order, area, school, name, appearance and speech, while Leyton found that the elaborate code of recognition used in Kildaragh depended most on schools attended and games played (Leyton 1974). At this point, however, the research dries up, leaving a number of unanswered questions: How accurate is the process of telling? What are its functions — to avoid or to facilitate conflict? On what occasions is it called into play? There has been virtually no research on these and allied questions.

Another under-researched theme is the incidence of mixed marriages between Protestants and Catholics — the interface between the two groups. The delicacy of the subject in Northern Ireland has made enquiry difficult. In Rose's survey two per cent of the married respondents had partners from across the religious divide, but twenty-six refused to answer the questions (Rose 1971, 508). Harris claimed that in Ballybeg there was an 'almost universal refusal to recognise kinship across the divide' (Harris 1972, 143), and that mixed-marriage couples often ceased church attendance — a conspicious act in the 1950s when her research was carried out. 'Intermarriage bridges no gaps,' she concluded. Leyton too has referred to 'the total pro-hibition of marrying Catholics' among Protestants in Aughnaboy (Leyton 1975, 57). However, research by Hickey and others suggests that these conditions are far from universal, and that cross-religious relationships may be more common in other places (Hickey 1984).

Barriers to polarisation

There is a general consensus in the academic literature, there-fore, that Northern Ireland is the arena for a fundamental and dysfunctional social conflict, and that it is between Catholics and Protestants. Even such broad generalisations, however, are subject to a number of important qualifications. Their common premise is that a crude picture of Protestants and Catholics in stratified conflict is misleading and inaccurate. Barritt and Carter, for example, having described some of the major divisions, went on:

There is, however, another side to the matter. The two com-

munities in Northern Ireland live side by side, generally at
peace. Their people are linked by many ties of personal
friendship, and by occasional significant ventures in co-
operation . . . On the whole, people manage to adapt themselves very well to ancient and continuing differences, and
they use those differences to add to the richness and humour
of life.   (Barritt and Carter 1972, 2)

In some cases the qualifications amount to footnotes to the
broader generalisations — a question of fine tuning. In others
they fundamentally question whether the generalisations, in
their original form, are even a useful basis for sociological
investigation. Three factors in particular challenge the simple
immutable Catholic-Protestant dichotomy — the considerable
geographical variety in community relationships; the
alterations through time in the relationships; and the evidence
that neither group is cohesive.

Following an analysis of anthropological research in
Northern Ireland, Donnan and McFarlane drew attention to
the wide variations in the nature of Catholic-Protestant
relations throughout the province: 'As our review shows, there
seem to be some contradictory findings even within the body of
literature discussed' (Donnan and McFarlane 1983, 134). Some
of the contradictions are contradictions only if it is assumed that
Northern Ireland can be regarded as a unitary social entity. In
some important respects this might be questioned. Protestants
are more concentrated in the eastern part of the province along
the Lagan valley and counties Antrim and Down, while
Catholics predominate in the border areas, although even this
gives a false impression. It is rather more accurate to regard
Catholics and Protestants as living in a series of denominational
enclaves. In some cases, like the working-class districts of Belfast
described by Boal, there is a very high level of segregation; elsewhere, especially in rural areas, the enclaves may vary in size
from small groups to individual families. Poole's studies of the
small towns which are such a common feature throughout
Northern Ireland, show convincingly that the highly segregated
ghetto is untypical, and that in most parts religion is not a major
determinant in housing choice. Total absence of cross-religious
contact, therefore, is very rare; contact takes place in every part
of the province.

Community studies confirm this fragmented picture. Certainly Harris found that the closeness of kinship ties in Ballybeg, and the high correlation between religion and kin, reduced the incidence of cross-religion contact. However other researchers like Kirk found specific conditions in their communities which encouraged visiting and social contact. Yet another social pattern was described in Burton's study of urban Anro, which was adjacent to almost exclusively Protestant districts, but which housed virtually no Protestants. Leyton's Aughnaboy presented a Protestant mirror image, but in a rural setting. In effect all the major studies of particular communities described systems of relationships between Protestants and Catholics which were apparently quite distinct in their operation.

Because of the longevity of conflict and violence in Northern Ireland some commentators have been persuaded that one of its major features has been its immutability. The most direct recent expressions of this view have come from political scientists. Richard Rose has suggested that the basic lack of consensus about the legitimacy of the state is an almost insurmountable barrier to settlement. Aunger argued that the major splits in Northern Ireland were all congruent with the central divide between Protestants and Catholics, that this made cross-cutting allegiances and compromises difficult, and that this situation has altered little through time. The main challenges to these views have come from historians and social scientists. Historians have pointed out that relationships between Protestants and Catholics have not always been sharply dichotomous, and that allegiances have occasionally shifted in the past. During the last two decades of the eighteenth century, for example, Catholics and Presbyterians found common cause in the United Irishmen, until their attempted rising in 1798 failed. In 1932 Catholics and Protestants joined in a protest hunger march.

Although these instances were rare, there have been a sufficient number of similar illustrations (the 1965 cavalcade from Derry to protest about the location of Northern Ireland's second university, for example) to demonstrate that exceptional mutual feelings of deprivation can overcome sectarian suspicions. Community violence in Northern Ireland appears to have been cyclical rather than cumulative, and adjustments made during violent stages in the cycle have often been re-adjusted during more peaceful periods.

So the relationships between Northern Ireland's two religious groupings, rather than remaining static, have constantly changed. These changes have accelerated during periods of violence, and are more volatile in urban areas. Their effects may be altered again during peaceful periods, and have hardly affected many parts of the province at all.

In general, the importance of understanding the process of change — in determining the timing of social reforms, for example — has been underestimated in the social science literature.

So has the amount of internal division in both Catholic and Protestant communities. The wide variation among Catholics about their constitutional preferences is well established and has already been noted. Among Protestants, antipathy to Irish unification is a strong unifying factor, although opinion is more divided on the question of the political role which Catholics should have within Northern Ireland. The occasional tensions between the different Protestant denominations, it has often been suggested, were infrequent and unimportant. There is evidence that, before the First World War at any rate, 'the Protestant denominations as a whole shared a common mind, and the laity in particular ... were Protestants first and members of their own church after that' (Megahey 1969, 63). His opinion was shared by Emrys Jones:

> Any discussion of religious groups in Belfast is dominated by the fact that the population is sharply divided into Protestants and Catholics. Differences between denominations within Protestantism tend to be overlooked or dismissed; comparisons and contrasts are constantly framed in terms of the two major groups.   (Jones 1960, 172)

More detailed examination of the Protestant community, however, reveals important denominational rivalries. Nelson (1984) provided the most comprehensive analysis of political differences among Unionists, but Kirk (1967) showed that religious disagreements were often just as bitter and enduring. These tensions were also observed by Harris (1972) and Leyton (1970). Class was another factor which cut across the main Protestant-Catholic division. Jackson expressed this bluntly, in reference to both parts of Ireland:

> Let us be quite clear, the problem is one of the working class. There have been no riots in the prosperous areas of Belmont or the Malone Road in Belfast. (Jackson 1971, 3-4)

While Jackson may have exaggerated the sharpness of class differences, his implication that Protestant-Catholic relationships are generally different among middle- and working-class communities has been supported by other researchers. Both Kirk in Lurgan and Harris in Ballybeg observed that social mixing across the religious divide was almost entirely confined to middle-class settings — golf and tennis clubs, formal dances etc. — where a superordinate goal or interest cut across religious barriers. The fact that urban middle-class housing, as well as housing in general in many parts of the province, is more likely to be integrated may have contributed to the formation of common interests. Whatever the reason, there has been a high correlation between integrated housing and the absence of overt community violence.

3.

The Communities

THE FOCUS of this research is on two closely intermeshed themes, one immediate and empirical, the other fundamental and theoretical. The empirical aim is to examine the process and immediate effects of intimidation on people who were forced to leave their homes. The theoretical aim is to examine how relationships are regulated, modified or extinguished between the protagonists after the period of direct confrontation has passed.

The research was rooted in three particular communities in Northern Ireland which had suffered directly from the experience of intimidation — Kileen/Banduff and the Upper Ashbourne estates in Belfast, and Dunville. Thus the two themes are married: the inter-community confrontations which gave rise to intimidation in these communities is the empirical focus which is designed to throw light on the process of accommodation during the post-intimidation years.

No claim is made that the three selected communities are representative of Northern Ireland. On the contrary, they were selected from a specific population of communities which had experienced exceptional levels of violence through intimidation. This population had been identified in research carried out in 1972-3, which went some way towards establishing the general dimensions of intimidation, not only in Belfast, but in three other towns (Darby and Morris 1974). Indeed the variety which it revealed between different settings provided the basis for selecting the three communities; more directly, the two Belfast communities examined in this research benefited from the background established in the earlier study, although the greater part of the data was collected since 1982.

The selection of the three communities was determined by three main considerations:

1. The need to examine different experiences of intimidation
It was known from the earlier research that the ratio of intimidation between the greater Belfast area and the rest of the province was approximately 2:1 (62.2 per cent of all cases of intimidation reported to the police between 1973 and 1979 were in greater Belfast) and that there were significant differences in rural and urban experiences. Dunville was selected from the rural areas which had been badly affected as one which would illuminate some of the important differences, including the greater likelihood that demographic adjustments were accomplished without violence outside Belfast (see Darby and Morris 1974, 66-71). The two Belfast communities represented two different forms of intimidation; Upper Ashbourne's evacuations had mainly resulted from one short violent period, while Kileen/Banduff's experience went on for more than five years.*

2. The need to build in a longitudinal element
The present research was completed in 1984. Most of the Upper Ashbourne evacuations took place in 1970; Kileen/Banduff's movements went on from 1970 until 1976; and Dunville experienced its intimidation in 1981. Consequently the three areas had periods of fourteen, eight and three years to recover from their experiences, and it was possible to examine the effect of a period of stability on community relationships.

3. The need to examine districts which had experienced a variety of forms of intimidation
The three main forms of intimidation identified in the 1972-3 research — direct violence, direct threat and environmental threat — were all important to the research aims. The three communities were selected to allow study of all three forms.

As a result of these considerations, the three communities selected for study were Kileen/Banduff, the Upper Ashbourne estates and Dunville.

---

*In this book, place names specific to the study have been changed to protect some sources. Other references to places in Northern Ireland remain unaffected.

Kileen/Banduff

The Northern Ireland Housing Trust began the construction of the Kileen/Banduff estate during the 1960s, before the outbreak of the current political violence. At the time the only other public housing estate in the vicinity was a small development immediately south of it across the Montford Road, known as the Old Banduff estate, which had been built in 1952.

The location of the estate outside Belfast's city boundaries was the result of two demographic trends, one a gradual post-war migration from the western to the eastern part of the province, and the other a metropolitan shift away from the overcrowded and decaying inner city towards new suburban estates. More specifically, plans had been published for the redevelopment of large tracts of inner Belfast, and these were premised on the belief that the redesigned city centre would be incapable of accommodating its former population. Consequently a number of new suburban public housing estates were planned to hold the surplus.

The tenants who moved into the new Kileen/Banduff estate during the four years of its construction reflect the different stages of redevelopment which had been reached when each section of the estate was completed. Thus the southern part of the estate, around Montford Road and Acre Drive, had a disproportionately high number of tenants from the Protestant Taughmonagh, Sandy Row and Donegall Road areas. The northern part, that closest to the Hollow Road and which was completed in 1969, was populated mainly from the Catholic lower Falls Road and Andersonstown. These areas were largely exclusive in religious terms and included parts of the city which had long traditions of sectarian violence. A survey conducted in 1970, just after the estate had been completed, found that forty-five per cent of the Catholic families on the estate came from the Falls Road area, and that forty-eight per cent of the Protestant families had originally lived in the Shankill and Donegall Road areas of Belfast (Williamson 1970).

The connections between the families from these new colonies and the mother district from which they came are still very close. The discos in Finaghy Road south, two miles away, were still favourite haunts of young Protestants from Banduff in 1984.

The religious composition of the estate had been a central concern from the start, and the Housing Trust favoured a policy of religious integration. Consequently families of both religious groupings were given tenancies in all parts of the estate, although a tendency towards religious separation developed as building progressed. By an undramatic process of changing tenancies, the southern part of the estate became predominantly Protestant and the northern part largely Catholic. Between the two there was considerable mingling of the two groups. Despite this tendency towards polarisation, there was a degree of religious integration in all parts of the estate until 1970.

During the following six years, however, Kileen/Banduff experienced severe and persistent violence and intimidation which reshuffled the population of the area into two exclusive districts. By the time the worst of the violence had passed in 1976 the Montford Road divided a large Catholic estate, Kileen, and a small Protestant one, Banduff.

Eight years later the divisions created by the violence were still evident. Graffiti identified local loyalties: in Banduff, attacks on a local supergrass appeared alongside general support for the UDA and UVF; to the north of Montford Road, painted messages proclaimed that Kileen supported the Provisionals, exhorted British soldiers to go home, acclaimed the hunger strikers of 1981 and the Maze escapees of 1983, and wished success to Argentina in the international confrontation which was clearly not the World Cup.

There were just under 250 residences — flats, terraces and semi-detached houses — in Banduff, twelve of them bricked up and unoccupied in mid-1984. An internal report to the Housing Executive described it as 'geographically isolated', and concluded that the 'complete polarisation of the two communities' had 'catalysed the deterioration of the area' (Northern Ireland Housing Executive 1983). Kileen had more than 1,200 households of a more settled appearance, although the northern part of the estate, around Temple, was rather more unkempt and was less popular with tenants. Both were designated by the Executive as 'priority estates', indicating an urgent need for major structural or planning alterations.

The general area had no major industrial employers, although many women in Kileen worked in a large hospital some distance outside the district. Unemployment was high, estimated at between thirty-five per cent and fifty per cent by local community and social workers. It was particularly high in Temple and Banduff, the extreme northern and southern parts of the area.

The high number of single-parent families, some the result of imprisonment, also contributed to the poverty of both parts of the estate. However the social problems which most concerned local residents were those affecting young people. Doctors confirmed that problems associated with alcohol and drug addiction were increasing. Even more worrying for some parents was the relatively new attraction of teenagers to joyriding which had led to damage to property, injuries and even deaths in the area. The general lawlessness had created a youth subculture which seemed to most people to be increasingly uncontrollable. Parents associated this development with the chronic shortage of jobs for young people in west Belfast. Hence the Shamrock Workshop, which provided the only local job training opportunities, accepted young people from both Banduff and Kileen and was one of the institutions in the area supported from both sides of the sectarian divide.

The vast majority of children in Kileen/Banduff attended denominational primary schools close to the area, but had to travel for their secondary schooling. With very few exceptions Catholic children attended St Luke's boys' or girls' primary schools in upper Kileen. All the Protestant children went to Banduff primary school. The populations of all three schools had been severely affected by the evacuations and arrivals of the early 1970s. The combined total of pupils attending the two Catholic schools had more than doubled in three years, increasing from 652 in 1969 to 1,518 in 1972. Banduff primary school, on the other hand, had experienced a decline from 868 in 1969 to 161 in 1983.

Although teachers claimed that indiscipline and violence in the schools were not exceptionally high, these population changes had a number of other effects on the schools. The shrinkage in Banduff primary school, which showed signs of levelling off in 1983-4, had changed the status of the headmaster to that of a teaching principal, and had meant that substantial parts of the building were no longer used. In an attempt to make use of the site and to hold on to staff, a nursery school had been opened.

As alternative nursery provision was almost totally absent

from the area, the nursery school had persuaded some Catholic parents to send their children. By 1983-4 Catholics formed a substantial majority in the nursery school. Indeed the school authorities, while welcoming any development which allowed them to hold on to teachers, had taken the unusual step of limiting the proportion of Catholic to Protestant pupils to the ratio 3:1. In this way they attempted to hold the delicate balance between the need to maintain Protestant Banduff and the need to maintain the school population at a viable level.

As a result of their dramatic growth in the early 1970s, St Luke's boys' and girls' schools in Kileen had been forced to educate half their children in temporary classrooms since 1970. In 1983-4 half the children in the girls' school were still being taught in temporary premises, although the number of pupils had begun to level out by the mid-1970s and to decline since 1980. The recent decline partly reflected changes in the age structure of the estate and the growing stability of its population. In the opinion of a local clergyman, the stability also accounted for the high proportion of young people attending colleges of higher and further education.

The almost inevitable response of residents to questions about amenities in the area was that there were none. Certainly the absence of commercial leisure facilities like cinemas and dance halls, observed by Jenkins in another Belfast estate, was also marked in Kileen/Banduff (Jenkins 1983). Nevertheless two active community centres were organised by Belfast Corporation in Catholic Kileen, although residents of the smaller Protestant Banduff estate, in which there were no such centres, regarded them as alien and were not prepared to use them. The three public houses on the edge of Kileen were rarely used by people from Banduff. For the most part, Banduff drinkers favoured pubs outside the area in south Belfast.

Sporting facilities were also available close to, but outside, the estate for both Catholics and Protestants. The Gaelic Athletic Association (GAA) owned a large open area beside Kileen with three playing fields and four club houses; Andersonstown Leisure Centre was within walking distance. Protestants in Banduff also had access to playing fields along White's Road.

There were no shops in Banduff and only a few small ones in Kileen. Families with cars often fetched their weekly shopping from large supermarkets outside the district, using local shops to 'top up'. However people from both Catholic Kileen and Protestant Banduff made common use of shops along the Montford Road, on the boundary between the two parts of the estate; these included a chemist, butcher, post office, minimarket and co-op. Indeed one feature of both Kileen and Banduff was that all major facilities were outside the estates or on their edges. Both lacked any central focus, although the two community centres in Kileen provided resources for some interest in the estate.

With the exception of one Protestant and twelve mixed-religion families, every family living in Kileen in August 1983 was Catholic, in name at least. The claim by local clergymen that attendance at Sunday mass was around sixty-five per cent may seem large, but contrasts with Rose's 1968 survey which found that ninety-five per cent of Catholics in Northern Ireland attended at least once a week (Ross 1971, 496). It was also considered a considerable overestimate by some residents.

At the same time there were no Catholics living in Banduff. The majority belonged to the Church of Ireland, with Presbyterians the second largest denomination. Church attendance for all denominations was low. Although the Methodist congregation in Banduff was small, the Methodist church on Montford Road was the only Protestant church within the estate itself. This helped to explain the much greater involvement of Methodist clergymen in the affairs of the area, especially during the 1970s.

Levels of community violence in the area had diminished greatly since the mid-1970s. There was an army post/police station at Carrytree on the Montford Road, on the border between Catholic and Protestant localities. Occasionally the army and police patrolled the area. Some Protestants regarded the general security as inadequate, but the predominant view in Kileen was that police help was only sought with reluctance. The army was regarded with either neutrality or hostility in Kileen, and adopted a deliberately low profile. The result was that, apart from occasional skirmishes between youths and exceptional periods of tension such as the hunger strikes, Banduff and Kileen had experienced little community violence since 1976.

The Upper Ashbourne Estates

The Upper Ashbourne estates cover a butterfly-shaped wedge of land on the edge of north-west Belfast. They stretch for about a half mile between the Ashbourne and Jackstown roads. To their north, the steep and inhospitable sides of the Black Mountain have so far frustrated planners, despite the local severe housing shortage.

Within this area are four distinct estates — Everton, Vestry, Avoca and New Hull. The area is not regarded by its residents as a natural unit, nor has it ever been. On the contrary it is one of the parts of Belfast where the boundary between the two religious communities has been sharp and, on occasions, confrontational. Everton and Vestry are exclusively Protestant; New Hull and Avoca exclusively Catholic. The Vestry Road marks the frontier between them.

Everton, built in the early 1950s, was intended primarily as housing for the expanding Shankill district of Belfast, which lay to the east. As a result it was predominantly though not exclusively occupied by Protestants. When New Hull and Avoca were built, however, the religious demography of the area had altered. Certainly they were regarded as a further extension of Protestant west Belfast. However Catholic west Belfast, along the Falls Road, had expanded at an even more rapid rate. The building of the large Kellytown estate, which soon became almost exclusively Catholic, marked out the south of the Ashbourne Road, opposite New Hull/Avoca, as Catholic territory. In effect Protestant west Belfast had been outflanked by Catholic west Belfast. The collision point between the Protestant thrust from the east and the Catholic thrust from the south was the new estate of New Hull/Avoca.

These developments are clearer in hindsight than they were to contemporaries, and there was little evidence of sectarian tension when the estate was built. Indeed New Hull was predominantly Protestant. In 1963 the Controlled (Protestant) Stanley Primary School opened its doors, but there was no demand for the building of a Voluntary (Catholic) Primary School — a sure indication that there were few Catholics in the estate. In 1964 the Catholic proportion of New Hull was estimated at six per cent, and their children attended schools outside the estate.

Between 1964 and 1968 the Protestant majority in New Hull/Avoca declined from ninety-four per cent to about sixty per cent (Darby and Morris 1974, 41). By mid-1969 this had dropped to fifty-three per cent (Poole 1969). There is no strong evidence, either from contemporary news-sheets or from the memory of ex-residents, that this gave rise to apprehensions among Protestants. The reasons for departure were mundane — dissatisfaction with heating in the houses and high transport costs to the city centre. One Protestant family, for example, left in 1967 because New Hull was 'in the middle of the country — too far away from our friends'. The significance of the changes was not so much that Protestant families were leaving but that Catholic families were replacing them. As there was no similar trend in Everton/Vestry to the east, the 'frontier' position of New Hull/Avoca for Protestants may have been a subsidiary reason for the gradual shift in the estates' religious ratio.

Housing was the dominant concern of North Ashbourne residents in 1984. Although the majority of houses in the area were rented from the Housing Executive, most had been built by Belfast City Council before the Executive was formed. There had never been a comprehensive plan for the area. Consequently each estate was appended to the previous one as the city's housing needs expanded, presenting a cycle of housing styles stretching over forty years. The oldest houses were in Everton to the east, and were mainly terraced or semi-detached houses. Everton has remained substantially unaltered since the 1950s. In the northern part of Vestry estate too, flats have been demolished but not replaced by new buildings; in the southern part, some houses have remained unoccupied since their evacuation twelve years earlier. The atmosphere was one of suspended development, but without any compensatory hope of improvement.

Across the Vestry Road, in Catholic Avoca, housing conditions were even worse. In addition to circumstances peculiar to Avoca itself — drainage deficiencies which had caused raw sewage to surface in streets and houses, poor planning, damp and ill-constructed flats — the estate suffered from its position on the periphery of Catholic west Belfast, where overcrowding was serious. In Avoca, however, twenty-five per cent of the households were squatters in 1982, although some have since been legalised. The high proportion of squatters contributed to the instability of Avoca, and many tenancies were short. The presence of so many unoccupied houses in Avoca during the late 1970s and early 1980s, despite the general overcrowding in west Belfast and the high level of squatting in the estate, was the strongest illustration of its appalling housing conditions.

A 1974 study of social malaise in Belfast, which examined ninety-seven urban zones, confirmed that the highest level of overcrowding — an average of 1.38 persons per room — was in New Hull/Avoca (Boal, Doherty and Pringle 1974, 58). By 1983 this had deteriorated further. A report prepared for the Housing Executive concluded that 'the estate of Avoca is generally in an extremely dilapidated state' (see NIHE, no date, 7.6). The minister with responsibility for the Environment, after touring the estate, announced that 'he had found conditions in parts of it to be unacceptable, and had asked the Housing Executive to increase their efforts to improve general living conditions' (Sope, January 1983). Apart from overcrowding, there were serious structural faults in Avoca's flats and maisonettes as well as dampness, unsatisfactory electrical wiring and inadequate heating. Most serious of all were the sewage problems which had become apparent in 1974 and which flooded the Save the Children playschool in February 1981. A report to the Housing Executive conceded that there were 'recurrent blockages in the sewers in both the Avoca and New Hull estates', but went on to add that 'it must be stated, however, that tenant abuse is a critical element of the problem' (NIHE, no date, 6.3 and 6.6). Local people believed that the high level of gastroenteritis in the estate was a consequence of this, a view supported by a local doctor who described the area as a 'biological time bomb', and declared that seventy-five per cent of Belfast's hepatitis cases originated in New Hull/Avoca (Sirockin 1982, 3). A campaign on these issues by the Avoca Housing Action Committee, which had been formed in 1980, led to the demolition of seven maisonette blocks by 1984 and eventually to an agreement that all the blocks would be demolished.

So, in terms of both religious segregation and environmental deprivation, the Vestry Road was an epicentre for the area's difficulties. The farther away from it on both sides, the lower were sectarian apprehensions and the better the housing conditions.

Apart from a timber yard and an engineering works there were no large scale employers in the area. Unemployment rates were exceptionally high. As early as 1974 male unemployment in New Hull/Kellytown stood at thirty-three per cent, by far the highest in Belfast; Everton/Vestry, with a rate of 9.5 per cent, ranked twenty-second. The disparity between the two neighbouring estates arose largely from the availability of employment for Protestants in the Shankill district and the shipyards, and from the fact that the local large engineering firm had only 120 Catholics on its workforce of 8,500 in 1971 (Boehringer 1971). Unemployment in the area has risen considerably in the intervening decade. In 1982 it stood at between sixty-eight per cent and eighty per cent in Avoca and well over thirty per cent in Everton/Vestry (Moyard Social Survey, and local estimates). The poverty, even of those who were working, is illustrated by the high number of children qualifying for free school meals — seventy-five per cent of all pupils attending Stanley and Dunnock primary schools in 1983.

Teenagers formed a very high proportion of the population. The absence of amenities for young people, combined with general dilapidation, absence of effective policing and the attraction of paramilitary involvement, had led to an increase of vandalism and anarchy in the estates. Parents and teachers shared this perception and worry. Glue sniffing, drugs and alcohol were available to children from a very early age. Hijacking of cars was common. Young gangs were feared by older people.

In 1972 Sue Jenvey suggested that the pressure on parents and children to embrace membership of their common sectarian community had reduced the frequency of normal 'generation gap' family disputes. Her study of young people in Belfast at the start of the Troubles concluded:

> One of the major effects of living with the Troubles has been to direct the young away from rebellion against the adult world, characteristic of their age group, towards conformity with their parents and the local community.
>
> (*New Society*, 20 July 1972)

A decade later there was little sign of this in the North Ashbourne estates. On the contrary, the peer group held a dominant influence over young people in both Catholic and Protestant communities, to the concern of some parents. If this has emerged since Jenvey made her observations, it appears to have been a consequence of the increasingly closed communities into which teenagers have been locked by the Troubles. In one New Hull family the parents did not permit the teenage boy to leave the house after 7.00 p.m. except in their company, to avoid both military harassment and paramilitary involvement. While this may be an exceptional case, there was wide awareness of the dangers facing stray teenagers found in hostile areas, and parents often warned their children against leaving the estate. The teenagers themselves were often aware of the risk, and conformed. The result, according to one local teacher, was a diminution in their development:

> They are born and grow up in this estate. They go to church here. Their outside experiences are often limited to a taxi drive down the Falls Road. All this shows up in school. Their vocabulary, for example, is very limited. I place great importance on trying to broaden their world by giving them outside experiences — holidays, day trips, even a visit to the post office.

The high number of single-parent families in North Ashbourne was both a cause and a result of social deprivation. Rapid turnover of tenancies makes precise estimates difficult. In Avoca, however, twenty-seven per cent of the households had only one parent in 1982, and clergy and social workers agreed that the figure was well over ten per cent in the other estates (Moyard Social Survey). They also believed that the problem was not eased by the Housing Executive's allocation policy which encouraged an accumulation of the most deprived in unpopular estates. Fourteen years of violence had created new categories of single-parent families: people in prison as a result of paramilitary involvement, people 'on the run' or 'on active service', refugees from supergrasses, and the partners of those who had died in the Troubles since 1969.

In 1984 the four estates, with a total population of more than 1,500 families, had a grand total of nine shops. For routine daily shopping, residents could choose between the three mobile shops which circulated parts of the area selling fruit, vegetables and general groceries, or shops on the periphery of the estates. Weekly shopping often meant travelling into town by bus or in the 'people's taxis' which separately served loyalist and republican areas. In all four estates there were complaints about high prices in local shops.

Recreational facilities were also inadequate. Apart from a few bleak squares of grass in Everton, there were no parks or play areas. In 1984, the construction of a large leisure centre close to New Hull provided the first sport and leisure facilities for that part of the Upper Ashbourne, but was not used at all by the residents of the Protestant estates. The opening in 1983 of a new youth club in New Hull, according to a local teacher, 'has made a tremendous difference in the atmosphere of the estate'. For younger children there were two mothers' and toddlers' groups — one organised by nuns and the other by the Save the Children Fund — and a playbus from the Voluntary Services Bureau. In the Protestant estates, Everton had an active and efficient community centre which provided a range of services across the age range, but Vestry has had to settle for a small neighbourhood servicing centre.

Public telephones were in short supply. In 1983, for example, there was only one in the whole of Vestry. There were no pubs in any of the four estates, although many were available both to the Protestant east and the Catholic west. People from Everton and Vestry went drinking in the pubs and clubs of the Shankill Road, where family connections were still strong. Even within each segregated community, considerable caution was exercised about drinking venues. Some New Hull residents avoided drinking in a neighbouring area, saying, 'We're not welcome there. We disagree with them on politics'. Others drank there quite freely.

It should be added that, however poor the environmental setting, however inadequate the flats and houses in some parts of the estate, however great the poverty or serious the problems facing young people, the whole amounted to even more than the parts. The cumulative and interrelated effects of these conditions have created a fortress of deprivation from which many could not escape through inability to clear rent arrears or for other reasons. The Housing Executive strongly denied accusations that it dumped 'problem families' into the area, but the charge itself misses the point. The real process was a filtering one, where the 'better families' could escape through the filter to other houses, leaving a residue of 'problem families' who could not escape. In some cases this has led to dependency and apathy, and a feeling among people who live there that they have little control over their conditions. Many were unaware of, or did not claim, grants and allowances like free school dinners to which they are entitled.

By 1984 the level of community violence had diminished but not disappeared. Tension rose during the hunger strikes in 1980 and 1981 and there were eight attacks on workers from Mackie's engineering works, and three casulaties, between 1973 and 1983. Nevertheless sectarian clashes had become rare, because members of the two communities had few occasions or opportunities to meet each other, and the no-man's-land between them had become a formidable physical and psychological barrier. Joint police/army patrols from the recently renovated and apparently permanent Montgomery army post/police station were frequent, but well protected. So confrontations between paramilitaries and the British army had reached a point similar to that during the war at sea in the early 1940s, when the defensive capabilities of one side were poised in balance with the offensive strength of the other. Local views suggested that the phony war of 1940 might be a more appropriate analogy.

Dunville

Dunville is close to the geographical centre of Northern Ireland, not far from Lough Neagh. Its population of just over 8,000 and its role as a regional centre are both characteristic of Irish towns.

It is also characteristic of many Ulster towns in its foundation during the Plantation of Ulster and in its subsequent history. After the defeat and flight of the Celtic earls in 1607, their lands were confiscated by the crown and distributed among loyal citizens from England, Scotland and Wales. Their undertaking required them to build a settlement, and the ten houses erected in the 1620s formed the basis of Dunville. In 1628 it was granted a patent by Charles I to hold a town market in a six-acre common area to the north side of the modern town.

After the 1641 rising against the Planters the town was accidentally burned to the ground by royalist soldiers, and a contemporary map shows only two habitable houses. The purchase of the land lease by the Stewart family, however, started a century of solid growth. A Presbyterian congregation began to meet in 1646, and an Anglican rectory was built shortly after. An ambitious plan to build a new town which would 'rival even the avenues of the metropolis' (i.e. Dublin) produced the creation in the 1740s of Dunville's most unusual physical feature — a 130-foot wide main street which stretches unbroken for over a mile, with side streets leading from it. By 1766 there were 595 families in Dunville, 427 Protestant and 168 Catholic.

During the nineteenth century Dunville developed the paraphernalia of a substantial town, with four churches, a dispensary, three inns and a number of shops. A linen and provisions market was held each Saturday, and a corn market on Tuesdays. Houses began to fill in between the side streets, and the production of linen provided work. By 1883 3,870 people lived in the town, and four factories employed 1,100 workers. The number of churches had risen to six and there were nine schools. The Great Northern Railway connected the town to places south of Lough Neagh, and the Belfast and Northern Counties Railway to the north. The town has no rail connections today.

Dunville's growth continued undramatically during the twentieth century. Textiles were gradually replaced as the main source of employment by a bacon factory started in 1938 and a cement production plant in 1968. However, the town's continuing growth — from around 5,000 in 1961 to over 8,000 in 1981 — was based more on its growing importance as an administrative and commercial centre than on industrial expansion. Nevertheless in 1981 it ranked only twenty-fourth of Northern Ireland's urban centres.

The growth of Dunville's population by twenty-three per cent between 1971 and 1981, and its continued expansion since then, was not due to a sudden rise in fertility. Indeed the under-15 age group actually fell by seven per cent, while the retired population rose by eight per cent (NIHE 1984). The main cause was an acceleration of the tendency for families to move from isolated farmhouses and villages into towns. During the late 1970s the Northern Ireland Housing Executive, for reasons of economy and 'rationalisation' of its services, actively encouraged this demographic shift. It became very difficult to secure planning permission for new rural buildings. The construction of 175 houses in new estates along Baptistry Road in south-east Dunville, and a further 104 at Oakgrove to the north-west, reflected a policy decision by the Executive to concentrate housing investment in the town. The tenants of these houses mostly came from Dunville's rural hinterland. There are more recent indications that the Executive has relaxed its urbanisation policy, but the published housing plan for Dunville points to further rural depopulation. Three hundred acres are zoned for housing in Dunville between 1984 and 1995, and the population is projected to grow to 11,000.

'Whatever they're coming in for, it's not work,' was the view of one council employee, and certainly the town's industrial base is insubstantial. There are few reminders of the linen industry. Food processing is one of the two large industries in the town; the creamery and cheese factory are stable employers, and in June 1984 the local pork processing factory announced an export-led expansion which would more than double its work force to over 500. The other main industry is concrete; in 1983 eight small firms associated with quarrying and concrete production — lime and cement works, concrete products, building suppliers — were advertising in the town's guide. Apart from these the only industrial employer in the town was a small engineering works, although a 20-acre industrial site was planned.

Unemployment in the town has been exceptionally high. During the late 1970s it rose even in relation to Northern Ireland's other depressed regions. From 1983 it has ranked second worst of the province's districts, after Strabane. In May 1984 the general unemployment rate stood at 36.9 per cent against Northern Ireland's 21.5 per cent.

Despite this there is an air of activity and modest prosperity about the town. This is a function of its position as a provincial centre, and the agricultural, commercial and administrative advantages that come from that. The mixed farming on good land surrounding the town not only supports the food processing factories but maintains a market yard in the town three days a week. One of Northern Ireland's three agricultural colleges is located at Hegarty two miles to the south, and the town's bucolic character is further demonstrated by its medical priorities: it has almost as many vets (five) as doctors (seven).

The Saturday market which was established in 1628 still operates in Dunville's main street and the town's shops have a prosperous appearance. Indeed the town's amenities are far superior to what its population would appear to justify. In 1984 there were four hotels, five licensed and two unlicensed restaurants, eleven cafés and nine bars and lounges, all indicating a substantial traffic from outside the town. The presence of at least fifteen garages reinforces the point. For entertainment the town has three cinemas, five weekly dances, five bookmakers and an impressive list of sporting facilities, including a modern swimming pool and squash courts, a bowling green, tennis courts, an 18-hole golf course and three football pitches. All of the sporting facilities, except the football pitches, are concentrated in the south side of the town around Waterford Road. The importance of siting facilities in areas acceptable to all major interests in the town is widely recognised, and a projected leisure centre will also be located on Waterford Road. These amenities contribute significantly to local employment and it is clear from interviews that they have also contributed to the town's recent expansion.

Employment has also been helped by the superstructure of administrative offices based in Dunville. As principal town in the Dunville District Council area, it is administrative centre for a number of smaller towns and villages, and the council offices are in the town. So also are the regional offices for four government departments. The Northern Ireland Housing Executive and Northern Ireland Electricity Services also have offices in the town. All of these provide salaried posts at both clerking and managerial levels. A recent analysis of Northern Ireland's social geography identified Dunville as one of four examples of towns which had a 'high proportion of managerial and professional people... presumably because of a different employment structure and greater residential integration' (Compton 1978, 133). The presence of a substantial middle-class managerial and professional population in Dunville, which gave the town a salary-based commercial prosperity despite its high unemployment rate, is more related to its administrative functions.

Two weekly newspapers have addresses in Dunville, the *Mid-Ulster Times* which has a largely Catholic readership, and the *Mid-Ulster Express;* only the latter has editorial offices in the town. The *Express* was founded in 1891 and has a circulation of just under 12,000. Although it declared itself to be 'apolitical and areligious' in its first issue, and still has no editorial, it is recognised locally as a paper for Protestants and unionists. All the births, marriages and deaths recorded in 1891 and 1942, for example, were Protestant (Cowan 1984), and the Orange parades on the Twelfth of July accounted for a third of the copy in the following issue in 1983. Its recent coverage of Gaelic sports and its contemporary correspondence columns indicate an awareness of a Catholic readership, and indeed in 1984 the editor was a Catholic.

Dunville was distinguished from many other Plantation towns by its relatively low level of residential segregation. Certainly there were streets and estates where one or the other religious group formed a majority, but none of these were exclusively unidenominational in 1980.

Nevertheless the ratio of Catholics to Protestants has been a sensitive issue for as long as many of its residents can remember. By the 1970s Protestants formed only a narrow majority in the town. Consequently the religious affiliations of the newcomers who sharply increased its population during the 1970s were keenly followed in the town. Their arrival indisputably nudged the Catholic minority in Dunville closer to numerical parity with the Protestants. In 1983 it was estimated by one of the Catholic priests that the population of All Souls parish had almost doubled in the preceding five years. In the same year the number of pupils in the two Catholic primary schools outnumbered the equivalent enrolment in the Controlled (Protestant) school by 847 to 788. In the absence of more recent and reliable data, opinion in the town reckoned that the Catholic proportion had almost reached parity by 1983, a position which had already existed in the district council area as a whole by 1971; in that year Dunville district was estimated to be 49.2 per cent Catholic.

A consciousness of belonging to distinct Protestant and Catholic communities, as well as to the same Dunville community, is particularly evident when questions of land ownership arise. 'There is an incredible protection of territory and property. Every inch is marked and remembered,' as one long time resident put it. A local politician expanded on the point: 'It's never discussed in public, but people around here don't like to see property going to the other side. Not many farms have shifted in my lifetime.' While this applies to agricultural, and to some extent to commercial, property, a local estate agent claimed that privately owned houses in the town are bought and sold on purely market criteria.

The other main arena for community discord was the question of local employment, and especially the patronage available to the local council. Although the reorganisation of Northern Ireland's system of local government in 1973 removed considerable powers from the control of councils, Dunville District Council still employed about seventy people during the 1970s. For most of the same period there had been eight Protestant unionist and seven Catholic nationalist councillors. A verbal exchange in the council chamber in 1981 demonstrates the rigidly partisan nature of its operations. Complaining about the fact that there were no members of the minority community on any council committee, the minority leader asked rhetorically, 'How do we get on these boards?' 'By winning the next election,' was the chairman's reply (*Mid-Ulster Mail*, 4 June 1981).

Charges of sectarian discrimination in employment were frequently made in council meetings. In 1977 an investigation by the Northern Ireland Commissioner for Complaints into the pattern of council appointments concluded:

> I found evidence in these cases that the two sides of the council had consistently voted for candidates of their own choosing along sectarian lines.

A second investigation was conducted by the Fair Employment Agency in 1980. This was a more comprehensive analysis of council employees and found significant imbalances between Catholics and Protestants:

Table 3.1
Religious Breakdown of Employees, Dunville D.C.

	Protestant		Catholic		All	
	N	%	N	%	N	%
Staff Grade	13	87	2	13	15	100
Manual Grade	42	73.7	15	26.3	57	100
Total	55	76.4	17	23.6	72	100

(Osborne 1982, 524)

The report was debated by the council and rejected by eight votes to seven, the familiar sectarian breakdown. The opposition claim that it was a 'damning indictment of the council' was countered by the chairman's claim that 'it's the greatest load of waffle I have ever seen' *(Mid-Ulster Mail,* 12 January 1981).

It may be significant that, before 1980, the issues which had most agitated community relations in the town — land ownership and employment — were both economic. Apart from these, and the public ritualised council exchanges, most local people claimed that relationships between Catholics and Protestants in the town were exceptionally cordial. The presence of a number of successful Catholic business families in Dunville was regarded as a significant factor in encouraging commercial co-operation in the town. Their strength, and their consciousness of it, allowed them to co-operate with Protestant shopkeepers to mutual advantage. The paramount importance of business, even over such sensitive matters as the routes of political demonstrations, was regarded as a conservative bonding force for the town.

Even during the growing violence of the 1970s — and Tyrone had its share of murders and atrocities — the town was remarkably unruffled by overt sectarian bitterness. In the Royal Ulster Constabulary's annual listing of reported cases of intimidation, 'M' district — in which Dunville, most of County Tyrone and part of County Fermanagh are included — ranked last or second last every year. In 1979 there was not a single reported case of intimidation in the entire division. When the town suffered its first serious violence and intimidation during the 1981 hunger strikes it was quite unprepared. The consequences of the resulting enforced population movements are not yet clear.

One popular view was that the evacuation of Catholics from Ranafast, and of Protestants from Clanmor to Oakgrove, has divided the town sharply and geographically across the middle. A clergyman and a council official independently believed that the northern part of the town had become Protestant, while the south was largely Catholic. This view that there was a 'line across the town' was exaggerated; the parish records of one large Protestant church in the town, for example, demonstrated a spread of parishioners in all parts of Dunville. There is evidence, however, that certain individual estates were becoming predominantly Catholic or Protestant. This process was not taking place by means of the dramatic and violent convolutions which had marked 1981, but by an unremarkable and gradual tendency for housing transfers to be partly affected by sectarian considerations. It would be a mistake to exaggerate it. Many parts of the town, including most of the privately owned houses, have been unaffected, and even those more recent movements which have taken place were more an effect of troubled times than of hostile acts directed against individuals.

It would also be a mistake to exaggerate the clarity with which one can describe all the inhabitants of Dunville as Catholics and Protestants. Clergy in the town remarked on its high proportion of mixed-religion families. Even if one disregards the claim by residents — not contradicted by people who lived there — that sixty-five per cent of the families in Rathbeg estate were mixed-religion, there has undoubtedly been a tradition of marrying across the religious divide which is not only unusual in a Northern Ireland context, but which has created a level of tolerance for the phenomenon in Dunville. The appearance of 'wrong' names on parish registers — Protestant O'Neills and Murphys and Catholic Larmours and Ballantynes — points to some level of ecumenical activity in the past.

Regardless of any tendency towards segregation in its living quarters, Dunville's commercial and servicing centre has been only marginally affected by the violence. 'The lines are a wee bit tighter now', according to one shopkeeper, but religion appeared to be a peripheral consideration when it came to choosing where to shop or drink. The local community relations policeman estimated that perhaps four pubs and two discos were 'Protestant' or 'Catholic' establishments, and it was rare for religious mixing not to take place in places of entertainment. Shopkeepers maintained that few people from the town made distinctions about where they spent their money, although country shoppers supported their co-religionists. 'There may be some tendency for people to favour friends,' as one put it, 'but for most people here the half-crown is more important than the crown.' There were occasional scuffles outside discos, and once outside two hotels, in 1981, but this died out soon afterwards. Just before Christmas 1983 the security gates which had blocked off the main street for more than ten years were quietly removed, and Protestant and Catholic tradesfolk both welcomed the return to normal commercial practices. The non-sectarian business interests of the town emerged from the events of 1981 largely unaffected.

4.

Intimidation:
The Problem of Definition

THE TERM 'intimidation' was used frequently by witnesses during the inquiry into the 1864 riots in Belfast. It was also a feature of Irish rural violence during the nineteenth century. Townshend has described the extent to which it was ingrained in Irish society at the time:

> A whole range of retributive actions was available, and the system of terror was so efficient that extreme violence was not necessary: the anticipation was enough to ensure compliance.
> (Townshend 1983, 22)

The effectiveness of using a threat, rather than actual violence, was rooted in the 'fairly high expectation of retribution if it were ignored' (Townshend 1983, 9). Townshend described this as 'enforcement terror'; it was used, not to make a gesture, but to produce an immediate effect.

The term 'intimidation' was not confined to Ireland, of course, and has been used in social science literature, especially in the American research about labour disputes and the Ku Klux Klan, as well as in research into secret societies like the Mafia (e.g. Hardman 1937). Despite this it has not been elevated to the status of a phenomenon with an agreed definition in either psychological or sociological literature. Most psychologists have been content to subsume it under such characteristics as 'fear' and 'threat', where the former is considered as arising from an immediate perception of danger and the latter as an anticipation of future danger. Within the social sciences the only definition discovered was in the 1937 edition of the Encyclopedia of the Social Sciences (Seligman 1937, 239-42), and the category was omitted in the subsequent edition (Sills 1968). The 1937 definition, by E. Hardman, was clear:

Intimidation as a means of achieving desired ends is a feature of behaviour where power or authority is based primarily and essentially on force. The less the public feels bound by stand-ardised ethical norms of conduct, the larger are the oppor-tunities for using intimidation.   (Hardman 1937, 239)

Hardman went on to incorporate group activities within his definition, drawing particular attention to minorities in Europe and Negroes in the southern United States in 1937. He also pointed out that 'a whole social group may practise intimi-dation upon another group' (Hardman 1937, 241). The main weakness in his definition, however, was his exclusive emphasis on physical force and subsequent failure to consider the impor-tance of threat, and his failure to consider, as part of the process, the perceptions of the threatened individual or group.

Working within this background, and from the use of the term in the Irish context over the last century, it is possible to move towards a tentative definition of intimidation. The main problem is whether it should be defined by the intention of the intimidator, the action of the intimidator or the effects on the victim. Certainly intimidation suggests an intention to produce certain responses from the victim, but if the determination is not manifested in some form of action — a threat or an act of violence, for example — it remains fixed among such psychological concerns as prejudice and stereotyping. A prejudiced attitude may not lead to prejudiced behaviour, some sociologists believing that, on the contrary, 'behaviour typically shapes and alters attitudes' (Raab and Lipset 1971, 35). Further, unless the threat or action leads to some response from the victim, it is indistinguishable from the everyday abuse common in divided societies. So it is a premise of this research that intimidation requires action rather than intention, and should be defined by both the actions of the perpetrators and their effects on the victims.

In Ireland, on the basis of the history of violence since 1835, intimidation has been confined to two main areas. The first was pressure on people to move from their workplaces. The attacks on Catholic workers in the docks and shipyards, and on factory workers from both religions, have been features of all major riots since 1857, and pubs and shops in hostile areas were prime objects for attack in 1886 and 1969. However, this has been a subordinate theme to the extensive and recurrent intimidation of people from their homes. This predominant form of intimidation involved a much greater variety of settings — minority families forced to evacuate hostile streets; mixed-marriage families pressured in both ghettoes; islands of families departing from alien neighbourhoods; even entire districts or housing estates changing in their religious composition, where demographic trends appeared to endanger the future security of whole communities.

In all these settings it is clear that the victim's perception of what was happening was as important in determining responses as the intention of the perpetrator. What was perceived as a direct threat by one person was sometimes dismissed as a chance occurrence by another.

For the purpose of this research, intimidation is defined as the process by which, through the exercise of force or threat, or from a perception of threat, a person feels under pressure to leave home or workplace against his or her will.

It can be considered within a framework of three categories, acknowledging that they are not initially exclusive, or discrete:

(1) actual physical harm;
(2) actual threat;
(3) perceived environmental threat.

1. Actual physical harm

The most effective and direct form of intimidation is the use of force. This is not always a crude, indiscriminating weapon, but incorporates three main forms of violence: damage or destruction of property; injuring or disabling; and death. It is possible to envisage the form of pressure moving systematically through these increasingly penal stages until the intended effect has been achieved.

Physical harm has taken a variety of forms during the Belfast riots from 1857 to 1969. Workers ejected from the shipyards or factories, or attacked while going to their workplace; pets and children beaten by other children because of family religion; husband or wife jostled or beaten; stones, bottles petrol bombs or bullets directed through windows or doors; houses and public houses ransacked whether vacant or occupied; furniture piled up in the street or burned; petrol bomb attacks resulting in damage or destruction to buildings; a member of the family shot, injured or killed. The list is almost endless, and has altered little since the events described in 1857.

2. *Actual threat*

The threat of physical harm falls just short of the use of force as an effective form of intimidation. It is designed to induce fear of physical danger. Although no violence or destruction has taken place, the threat is sometimes sufficient to persuade its victims to leave their homes or jobs. This type of psychological threat can take many forms, from a poison pen letter or anonymous telephone call to masked men calling at the door. Bullets have been sent in envelopes to minority families; in North Belfast in 1970 some Catholic families had mass cards posted to them; Protestant families have had slogans painted on their doors. This sort of pressure, like actual physical harm, is directed against specific individuals. It was one of the most common factors which caused housing movement.

3. *Perceived environmental threat*

The two categories of real physical harm and real threat are clearcut cases of intimidation, in that one person or group is trying to force an unwilling response from another. Beyond these lie the complex cases in which the perception of the victim plays a more important part than any objective personal threat. As with the other categories, this contains a wide spectrum of conditions. For the purpose of this research, they may be considered, however, in two main groups: specific environmental pressures and general environmental pressures.

Specific environmental pressures include a variety of conditions within one's immediate community which create a feeling of unease or an impression that intimidation might occur, even though no specific threat has been made: neighbours becoming unfriendly; children finding it more difficult to find friends; an increase in the number of political or sectarian slogans on pavements or walls. In their mildest forms these changes can convince parents that their district is no longer suitable for rearing their children. They can, however, also take forms which, while not directed at individuals, are symptoms of a more general violence in the community — families caught in crossfire between paramilitaries and army; houses in areas subject to frequent bombings. The desire for a more peaceful neighbourhood can be a powerful motivation for a family to leave its home.

General environmental pressures result, not from changes within a community, but from pressure on the community itself. These pressures have been strong enough to produce enforced population movements, not because individuals have been attacked or threatened, but because the communities to which they belonged have themselves become isolated and vulnerable. There are many examples of communities becoming detached from their broader religious heartland through gradual demographic changes. The Catholic enclave of Willowfield in east Belfast, or Protestant New Barnsley surrounded by Catholic estates, provide two instances where communities eventually disappeared as the result of perceived vulnerability within the broader urban setting. There is evidence that Catholics and Protestants have regarded their communities in such strategic terms since the 1835 riots, and have carefully monitored the shifting patterns of religious demography.

Both these latter groups are distinguished from the earlier categories in one important way. Intimidation which involved actual physical harm or actual threat is designed to force an unwanted course of action on their victims. In the case of perceived threat, the individual is not threatened, but feels insecure as a result of general factors operating within or outside the community. This is here described as environmental threat, and falls within the definition of intimidation in this research.

It is more difficult, however, to deal with the importance of the perceptions of victims, as distinct from observable external factors. In reality this distinction is not so easily sustained. There is substantial research evidence that the people most affected psychiatrically by civil violence are those with a history of mental disorder (e.g. Lyons 1971 and Heskin 1981), and clearly a person's decision to leave a house or job may be explained by perceptions of reality as much as by the reality itself. No sharp line exists between objective and perceived threat. Nevertheless, for the purpose of this study, individuals who leave their homes or jobs without evidence of physical attack, real threat or environmental threat are regarded as belonging to the province of psychiatric study, and are not included in the definition of intimidation.

The complex processes of intimidation, ranging from physical attack down to environmental intimidation, can be presented in the form of a composite model.

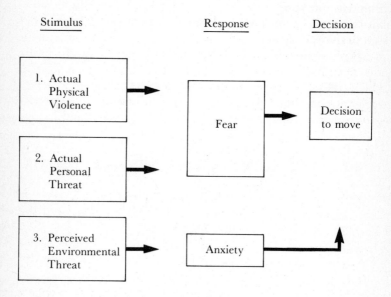

These categories, while useful for the analysis of intimidation, are far from discrete and may be regarded as a progressive process. The time likely to elapse between each stimulus and the decision of the victim is incorporated in the model; hence physical threat would seem more likely than environmental threat to lead to a decision to move. Whether or not the stimuli actually produce evacuation depends on the character and personality of the victim, as well as on his or her domestic circumstances. There have been many cases of neighbouring families, apparently intimidated to equal degrees, responding in quite different ways, some remaining and some departing.

There is a difference in kind between the first two categories and the third. In the first two a direct action against an individual target — whether violence or threat — is likely to produce fear, the reaction to an immediate danger. In the case of environmental threat, on the other hand, the response is more accurately described as anxiety, which is essentially anticipatory in nature, an attempt to cope with the future, however ineffectively.

So should environmental threat be considered as a form of intimidation? Is it possible to have intimidation without the intention of the aggressor to intimidate? The problem in answering these questions lies in measuring intent. What can be said in the end is that environmental threat was indisputably a major reason for some families leaving their homes, and that it was regarded as such by many evacuees. Any classification which rejects it ignores a factor which provides a better explanation of enforced population movement than an accumulation of individual acts of aggression. If it was not intimidation, it was a potent form of threat.

5.

Intimidation in the Communities

THE IMPACT of violence on Belfast in August 1969 was all the greater because it followed a long period of relative tranquility. The fact that two Belfast men were fined for intimidation on 7 August gave little warning of what was to follow (*Belfast Telegraph*, 7 August 1969). The ferocity of events on 14-15 August 1969, when Catholic and Protestant mobs clashed between the Falls and Shankill roads and five people were killed, had the added element of surprise. The British army was called in to restore order and erected a physical barrier between the Catholic and Protestant districts in the Falls/Shankill area, the first of many 'peace lines' throughout the city.

One consequence of the violence was the revival of intimidation in Belfast and the enforced population movements which accompanied it. There were three particularly severe periods between 1969 and 1972.

In the months of August and September 1969 a total of at least 3,570 families were displaced in the County Borough of Belfast, mostly from the west and north-west of the city. An analysis of 1,820 cases of families which appeared on official lists revealed that eighty-three per cent of those who moved were Catholic. To put it another way, about five per cent of Belfast's Catholic households vacated their homes in the late summer of 1969, some of them personally intimidated, many fleeing to the security of Catholic areas (Poole 1969).

June and July 1970 saw the movement of most of the 700 Protestants from the New Barnsley estate in West Belfast. This estate, while predominantly occupied by Protestant families, was isolated from other Protestant areas and increasingly surrounded by new Catholic estates. Direct intimidation certainly took place, but a general fear and feeling of vulnerability proved to be even more intimidating factors.

The third period followed the introduction of internment on 9 August 1971. A Community Relations Commission research unit recorded that 2,069 families had been forced to abandon their homes during the rest of the month. The concentration was in the western and north-western parts of the city, especially in Ardoyne, where two entire streets were destroyed by fire. The most significant trend observed in the movements of August 1971 was the re-sorting of mixed areas into segregated zones, and the continuation of the patterns of 1969 and 1970. Protestants who left their homes tended to move to 'safe' estates on the outskirts of the city and to other parts of the province. Catholics crowded into the already over-populated Catholic areas, especially west Belfast and the Short Strand.

It is impossible to determine accurately the total number of Belfast families who had been forced to leave their homes during these years. However one research investigation which attempted to do so concluded:

> Our estimate of the total enforced movements in the Belfast area between August 1969 and February 1973 is between 8,000 families (minimum) and approximately 15,000 families (maximum). Based on an average family size of four, the figure suggested by our investigation, this indicates a total of between 30,000 and 60,000 people who were forced to evacuate their homes — roughly between 6.6 per cent and 11.8 per cent of the population of the Belfast urban area.
>
> (Darby and Morris 1974, c)

There has been no systematic study of the rates of intimidation since 1974. The annual statistics published by the Royal Ulster Constabulary are an unreliable guide. Many cases — especially those with Catholic victims — were not reported. In 1973, the year in which the police statistics reached a peak of 3,096 cases, a grand total of seven cases were reported in west Belfast, which included the police stations at Springfield Road, Andersonstown and Hastings Street. Further, as the police themselves concede, 'nothing is more difficult to detect than a case of intimidation unless the perpetrator is caught in the act by the police or the victim gives full co-operation' (Chief Constable's Report 1974, 11). Nevertheless, if the police statistics in fact reflected some general trends, there was a steady decline in the number of reported cases, apart from an inter-ruption in 1977, the year of the Ulster Workers' strike, from 3,096 in 1973 to 446 in 1979. After that date, although the figures were analysed differently, the decline seems to have continued until 1984, when ninety-four cases of intimidation originated. Even the hunger strikes campaigns of 1980 and 1981 did not produce large-scale intimidation in Belfast. The indications are that the movements of the early 1970s had resolved the majority of territorial disputes in Belfast and clarified the divisions between the two communities.

It is even more difficult to assess the level and intensity of intimidation outside Belfast. The 1974 report remarked:

> The majority of towns in Northern Ireland have experienced little or no intimidation problems. This is particularly true of towns which do not have identifiably sectarian housing estates. (Darby and Morris 1974, 69)

Many towns were not polarised in this way, so it would have been difficult to apply collective pressure on a coherent minority. Even in some towns with segregated quarters and which had experienced intimidation — like Derry, Lurgan, Portadown and Armagh — housing exchanges were often amicably arranged through advertisements in local newspapers. According to the police, 'the majority of cases [of intimidation] were reported in the Greater Belfast area.... Country areas suffered least from this crime' (Chief Constable's Report 1976, 4). Outbreaks of intimidation in small towns and rural areas were characteristically associated with particular political crises or local unrest. During the Ulster Workers' strike in 1977 and the H-blocks campaign in 1980 and 1981, for example, a number of small towns had outbreaks of intimidation. In the main, however, intimidation was an urban phenomenon.

The religious breakdown of intimidation victims is the subject of dispute. The great majority of early population movements in Belfast were Catholic families, estimated at eighty-three per cent in 1969 (Poole 1969), sixty per cent in 1971 (NICRC 1971) and sixty-six per cent in 1972 (Darby and Morris 1974). The cases reported to the police during the 1970s were quite evenly divided between Catholics and Protestants: 'Both sides of the religious divide were affected almost to the same extent' (Chief Constable's Report 1975, iv). To confuse matters further, there were periods when there was considerable intimidation within each community rather than between them. During 1977, the year of the Protestant Ulster Workers' strike, eighty-five per cent of the cases reported to the police involved Protestant victims, many of them intimidated by other Protestants to support the strike.

Intimidation in Kileen/Banduff: 1970-76

The violence had both a general and specific effect on Kileen/Banduff. Naturally the rise in tensions throughout the city affected the estate. Catholics and Protestants still living there recalled the wild rumours of invading mobs about to march on the area, respectively from Lisburn and the Falls Road, intent on genocide: 'We thought that we were going to be murdered in our beds,' as one Catholic resident put it. For a period of about three weeks vigilante patrols were organised to protect the area. At the same time there was a public concern to hold together Kileen/Banduff and the neighbouring estates as a region which housed both Catholics and Protestants. Although the patrols reflected the religious composition of each locality, a central committee co-ordinated activities for the entire district. This met each night in the comfort of a British Legion hall, which conveniently had a licence to sell alcohol. There they received reports from the patrols, maintained contact with police and army and generally adopted the role and perks of a general staff. The years of patrolling were often recalled with nostalgia by people still living in the estate:

> It's true we had to get up at all hours of the morning, but we felt that we were doing something to hold the place together, instead of sitting at home in front of the TV. After a while I really enjoyed them. There were four on our patrol and we became real mates, although we didn't know each other all that well before the patrols. We used to bring beer and sandwiches with us and chat about football. The crack was really good. In fact the patrols went on long after any danger had passed. The boys in the British Legion [hall] were enjoying themselves so much they didn't want to stop.

The specific effect of the 1969 violence had much more serious consequences for the estate. Nearly fifty per cent of the families who had left their homes during August had lived in west Belfast (calculated from Poole 1969, 16), and many of them went to temporary accommodation in the same district — local schools, St Joseph's College of Education and temporary structures donated by relief organisations. Some moved into the houses of friends and relations in the northern part of Kileen/Banduff, which was still being constructed. The Housing Trust permitted some refugees to occupy unoccupied and even uncompleted houses and gave priority on its waiting list to intimidated families. The result was a sudden influx of Catholic families, many of them recent victims of violence, into the northern part of the estate. Some Protestants date the destabilisation of the estate from this time.

Although 1970 and 1971 were relatively quiet years for Kileen/Banduff, there was a gradual movement of Protestant families from the northern to the southern side of the estate, and some movement outside it altogether. They were replaced by Catholics. By 1971 the religious demography of the estate had hardened. Few Protestants remained to the north of Ardfoyle Drive; only a few Catholic families still lived south of Lucan Gardens; between the two there was still some level of mixing.

The mixing did not continue for long. Kileen/Banduff was one of the localities most affected by the movements which followed the introduction of internment on 9 August 1971. Ninety-eight families in the estate moved out of their homes, and 171 families moved in. Of the outgoing families eighty-nine were Protestant, thirty-two of them moving within the estate to the Acre Drive/Montford Road area. One hundred and forty of the new arrivals were Catholic, 126 of them coming from west Belfast (NICRC 1971).

These major shifts in the demography of Kileen/Banduff were accompanied by the first serious rioting in the area. Fighting between rival groups of youths became common, and the army established a post between the Catholic and Protestant districts in an attempt to stabilise the central part of the estate. The Northern Ireland Housing Executive, which had taken over responsibility for all the houses from the Housing Trust in 1972, supported the army decision by introducing a *de facto* policy of sectarian allocation of houses. An army report from this period concluded:

> Finally a peace line was established in 1971 across Kileen Avenue on the line of Ardfoyle Drive. The housing authorities tried from then on to allocate houses south of this line to Protestants and north of the line to Roman Catholics.
>
> (Field Regiment, 1972)

Far from stabilising the area, the army post soon attracted the attention of the Provisional IRA, who had been building up recruitment in the estate since the introduction of internment. Gun fights became more frequent and overshoots sometimes hit houses in the southern part of the estate. Protestants claimed that some families in the central Ardfoyle-Lucan locality were systematically harassed. Certainly most of the Protestants in these houses had moved out by the summer of 1972. The houses which they vacated became the focus for the next phase of demographic change.

Acknowledging that the 1971 peace line had become obsolete, the Housing Executive agreed to allocate the houses to Catholic families, some of whom were living with relations in the upper part of the estate. It was at this point that the Kileen/Banduff affair became more than just a localised fracas, and the confrontation became a public test of strength for the paramilitaries. The UDA, angry at what they regarded as betrayal by the Housing Executive, tried to prevent Catholics taking up the tenancies. The Provisional IRA was determined to extend the Catholic part of the estate and set a deadline for the occupation of the empty houses. The aim of the British army in the middle was to prevent change. The set-piece confrontation, when it came on 9 July 1972 in front of mass media attention, was indecisive, although it marked the end of a short IRA truce. In the end high politics and strategic considerations had outranked local interests, and the struggle between the IRA and UDA in Kileen/Banduff had become a microcosm for the Northern Irish conflict in general.

Between 1972 and 1976 tenants continued to leave the remaining Protestant part of the estate around Acre Drive. Protestants from other parts of the city were unwilling to move into vacated houses along what had recently been a well-publicised battlefield and where sporadic violence continued. The unease of those who remained was demonstrated by desperate pleas for support published in loyalist newspapers. In a news-sheet produced in south Belfast, for example, their beleagured situation was described as 'surrounded on all sides by republicans who are slowly but surely applying the squeeze, ably aided and abetted by the NIHE and championed by that obscene and obese Assembly man Paddy Devlin' (*Village UDA News*, 1973). More significantly the Official UDA newspaper, having outlined how 'the Kileen rebels and the Andersonstown thugs' were 'casting covetous eyes on the empty houses on the Protestant side', actually conceded that Banduff was 'a fringe area'. It went on to ask for support:

> We are quite determined to stay put, but we are still worried about the number of empty houses in the area and are anxious to get Protestant tenants for them. This is a good estate and we are a close knit loyal community that wants to stay that way. May I appeal to loyalists who wish to move from their present district to come and see us. We'd love to have you and you would be made welcome. Remember it was the Banduff loyalists who halted the rebels at Kileen. Come out and support us and help us fill those empty houses.
>
> (*UDA News*, 2, 5: 1973)

A contemporary army report confirmed the precarious position of the Banduff Protestants:

> There are many Catholic families in the relatively over-crowded area who would like to occupy these houses. The danger is that one day this might happen in which case there is likely to be retaliation from the Protestants.... The Housing Executive already have a policy to fill houses in the area as they become empty ... with uncontroversial tenants who are not deeply involved in a subversive organisation. It is believed that if suitable tenants can be found this will stabilise the population and enable those on the interface to live in peace.   (quoted in Murray and Osborne 1977)

The task proved impossible. Protestants continued to leave. The movement was undramatic, an erosion rather than an evacuation, but it included the main UDA leaders. By 1976 the

Acre Drive area, which had housed more the 200 Protestant families in 1970, had only about twenty remaining, concentrated in the western corner of Acre Drive. These were mainly old people who had watched their Protestant neighbours leave the estate and who felt very vulnerable. Although this enclave lasted for some time behind yet another peace line at the community centre on Acre Drive, its insecurity was heightened by what one Protestant described as 'a few set-piece riots'.

The departure of this Protestant rump from the estate was the result of one such disturbance. During the annual build-up of tension before the Orange processions on 12 July 1976, there were confrontations between rival crowds, shootings, stonings and rioting. On the evening of 13 July most of the remaining Protestant families were evacuated from the estate in one sudden and organised withdrawal. 'We were taken out in lorries,' as one ex-resident described it. X [a prominent local politician] was the leader and the UDA did the job.' Some of the Acre Drive houses were vandalised before they were abandoned. Toilets were smashed, paint strewn over walls and windows broken.

Seven years later there was still bitterness among some of the Protestant ex-residents of Acre Drive, who claimed that they had been forced to move against their wills by a combination of general hooliganism, IRA Pressure and the UDA 'panicking the people'. Within days of the UDA evacuations only one Protestant family remained to the north of Montford Road; in 1984 this family remained the single exception to the total segregation of the area. All the families who moved, some of them to temporary accommodation in Banduff primary school, were granted emergency status by the Housing Executive.

Since then Kileen became the general name applied to the Catholic territory north of the road. The small Protestant enclave south of the road, previously known as Old Banduff estate, came to be known simply as Banduff, demonstrating that the name had become associated with a religious community rather than the geographical unit which it had originally described. The people who lived there were uncertain about their future. 'We expected a big push across the road,' one resident said, and it looked as if their fears might be realised when Catholics moved into a row of houses on the Protestant side of Montford Road, numbers 112 to 120. They did not remain for long. The Housing Executive refused to confirm the tenancies, the army advised them that they could not guarantee their safety, and the UDA forced them to leave.

The occupation of these houses became a major concern for Protestants, mindful of the erosion of the earlier peace lines to the north. The Banduff Community Association was formed to help give cohesion to the area. The Housing Executive was persuaded to convert one of the houses into a community house. A number of mixed-marriage families, deliberately encouraged by the Methodist minister in an attempt to reduce antipathies, moved into the houses. Nevertheless the houses were unpopular, tenancies were brief and vandalism by the 'local cowboys' became a serious problem. By 1984 only a few of the houses were in use, one as a Citizens' Advice Bureau, one as a sub-office of the Housing Executive and one by the Banduff Community Association. The others were boarded up, and had been vandalised. As on Protestant community leader put it:

> ... The Catholics across the road can see the empty houses. What's to stop them going to the Executive and offering to occupy and renovate them? I wouldn't blame them, but it would be the end of us. . . .

The changes in Kileen/Banduff between 1969 and 1983 did not take place as a result of random acts of intimidation against individual families. The process of evacuation may have originally been the direct result of violence, but it set in motion a dynamic process which encouraged further departures. 'The better families leave first,' according to one ex-resident who clearly numbered herself among them, 'and the spineless ones follow them.' A Protestant community leader observed that 'the ones who are best equipped to hold the place together and provide leadership were the first to go'. Certainly the families who were last to leave Acre Drive, those transported by the UDA in 1976, were almost all old people. All this contributed to an atmosphere of collapse which encouraged the actual collapse that followed.

Nor can Kileen/Banduff be regarded in isolation from other parts of Belfast. The families who left the estate, and those who replaced them, believed that they had been intimidated from their homes. In many cases they were distraught, and bitter and nervous towards their enemies. Few were unaffected by their experiences. The principal of one school in the area described the condition of some of the children who had arrived at her school — hyper-nervous at any sudden noise, almost hysterical at the sight of soldiers, aggressive and withdrawn, in some cases children as young as five on sedatives. In time most of these symptoms disappeared. The point must be stressed, however, that intimidation in one part of the city set off shock waves which affected many others. In Banduff/Kileen one effect was the arrival of evacuees whose search for security did not include any general concept of 'community relations', or necessarily a willingness to live among members of the group which had expelled them from their homes.

In this atmosphere it was not surprising that many Protestants were convinced that the evacuations from the estate were mainly the result of the an IRA conspiracy. The obvious presence of Provisionals during the 1972 confrontation at Lucan Gardens, and during gun attacks on the army and on individual Protestants, lent support to this. For some Protestants the perception of IRA strategy was much more sinister. One believed that each Catholic advance in the estate was preceded by the deliberate occupation of houses in the interface area by 'hard-nosed Catholics', under instruction from the IRA; he described them as 'frontier families' willing to accept aggravation for the sake of the cause and willing to further the cause by creating further aggravation. Others described how streets emptied suddenly and an 'eerie silence' took over immediately before attacks on the army by the IRA. 'We were even able to tell the army when trouble was coming,' one Protestant leader claimed. This belief suggested that any real distinction between the Catholic community in general and the Provisional active service units in particular was meaningless.

In fact paramilitaries from both sides played a minor, if dramatic, part in events. Despite the publicity which attended the 1972 confrontation by the IRA and the UDA evacuation of Acre Drive in 1976, the total number of families who moved during these two events was no more than twenty-five. The other 180-200 families who left the estate went at other times, although no doubt affected by the drama. The pattern was one of a gradual erosion of the Protestant community, interspersed by short, public and violent set-piece confrontations. Protestants left Banduff less as a result of violence than to avoid it in the future.

Intimidation in the Upper Ashbourne estates: 1970

The enforced population movements which accompanied the violence of August 1969 were concentrated most heavily in west and north-west Belfast. According to Poole, who studied the movements of that year, 80.5 per cent of all evacuations came from those sectors (Poole 1969). The low level of evacuations from the Upper Ashbourne estates — one per cent of the families in New Hull/Avoca and even less in Everton/Vestry — therefore require some explanation.

No doubt the history of good relations in New Hull provides part of the reason, but this in itself was not enough to protect other tranquil communities. In fact there had been some fear that the violent conflicts further down the Falls and Shankill roads might threaten the district. This had led to the formation of the Ashbourne Joint Committee, which came to co-ordinate the activities of tenants' and community groups from the four estates and from the neighbouring estates of Turf Lodge and Kellytown. Its object was to prevent the stratification of the entire area into separate sectarian ghettoes, and at one time it supervised the patrolling of the area by more than 1,000 Protestant and Catholic vigilantes. It was a major factor in defusing tensions during 1969.

Although very few families left Upper Ashbourne in August 1969, large numbers of evacuees from other parts of the city arrived there. Temporary relief centres were set up in schools and other buildings. Most families soon moved on to more permanent accommodation, but there were still refugees in local schools when they opened in September. So an official emergency housing site was established in September 1969 to provide temporary accommodation for them. The site, which was located beside New Hull, had taken in thirty families by the end of October; by January 1970, 162 families were still in occupation. All of these had been recognised by the housing authorities as victims of intimidation.

These newcomers to the area created some unease among the

more permanent residents of the North Ashbourne estates.
According to one Avoca resident who had been active on the
Ashbourne Joint Committee:

> They were far more bitter than the rest of us. They didn't
> trust anyone. We thought we had done well to keep trouble
> away from the area, but the new people were not as moderate
> as us. But they couldn't be ignored. After all, they had
> suffered a lot, and there must have been thousands of them.

No data are available to measure exactly the demographic
shift in the estates between August 1969 and spring 1970, but it
appears to have been slight. According to both Catholic and
Protestant clergy, most families who did leave at this time were
Protestants, and they were replaced entirely by Catholics.

On Easter Tuesday 1970, however, the pattern was disturbed
abruptly. It is customary for some lodges of the Orange Order to
parade with bands during the Easter holidays, and also
customary for each procession to start at the house of the local
Master. In 1970 the Master of a local Orange Lodge lived in
New Hull estate, and the procession was planned to travel down
the Ashbourne Road past Everton and Vestry estates. However,
the sectarian violence of the previous year had sharpened
sensibilities and a hostile crowd began to gather on the
Ashbourne Road — mainly from neighbouring Kellytown.
Stones were thrown and windows broken in Protestant houses in
New Hull. One woman, then a child, remembered the scene
well: 'I saw my daddy crying. I never saw him like that in my life
before.' During the day a number of Protestant families left the
estate, mainly to the houses of relatives in Shankill and Glencairn
to the east, and to emergency accommodation in a neighbouring
school.

It was claimed by a number of Catholics and Protestants who
had lived in New Hull at the time that this evacuation was an
unnecessary overreaction, encouraged by outsiders. Two older
women, who moved to Vestry, claimed that the level of violence
was very low, a disturbance rather than a riot:

> We were nervous, though, and scared that things might get
> worse. All we needed was someone to tell us to keep calm.
> What we got were hooligans like Z [a well known loyalist
> politician] coming in and telling us we would have to get out.

There appears to be some justification for this view. There had been little sign of panic until the evacuation itself. Certainly the politician mentioned had played a prominent part in events, telling a number of families to move and providing transport. The operation itself, which required lorries for the removal of possessions, was speedy and efficient.

The form of pressure which led to the Easter moves was a combination of actual threats and a growing perception that New Hull's transformation into a Catholic estate was irresistible. The violence and threats were directed towards Protestants in New Hull as a community and did not discriminate between individual Protestant families. None of the interviewed ex-residents remembered any cases of Catholics from New Hull intimidating Protestant neighbours. Some referred to the absence of the 'responsible leaders' from the Joint Ashbourne Committee — Easter Tuesday is a popular holiday in Northern Ireland — to explain both the Catholic violence and the Protestant overreaction. The general view at the time was that the events of Easter Tuesday were unfortunate rather than cataclysmic, and most of the Protestants who departed soon returned. However this was followed, according to one man who did return, by a 'trickle of applications for transfers' to the housing authorities.

The return to relative normality was halted by a second outburst of violence on 12 July. The conditions surrounding it were remarkably similar to those of Easter Tuesday. Once again an Orange procession from New Hull produced a violent reaction from Kellytown; once again abuse and stones were directed from outside the estate towards Protestant houses in New Hull; loyalist politicians from outside the estate again became involved, again advised departure, and again provided transport. The atmosphere was described by one woman who, while experiencing no personal violence, had to leave the contents of her house behind when she fled; her belongings were delivered to her new address months later by the Welfare people, bundled into bedspreads and rotting:

> Everyone was saying, 'Are you going? I'm going.' We could hear the Kellytown crowd singing 'Run, rabbit, run'. As we left our neighbours were crying: 'Don't go; don't go.' But we were scared.

There were also differences between the Easter and July movements. The British army, a new element in the situation, attempted to intervene between the two groups and itself became the object of attacks from both. The main difference, however, was the duration and intensity of the hostility. The violence continued sporadically for a number of days and it became increasingly difficult for Protestants to believe that they could live peacefully in the estate. Some remained for months until alternative housing could be provided but by the end of the summer there were less than ten Protestant families in New Hull. Since Easter about 200 families had departed, and in October the demographic changes in the area were formally acknowledged by the departure of the Presbyterian minister from his house on the Kellytown side of the Ashbourne Road. His flock had left and his church hall, the Montgomery Memorial Hall, became an army post.

Considerable bitterness persists among some Protestants about the failure of their leaders either to support or defend them. For the political leaders the issue was simply one of defensible and indefensible territory. The encroachment of Catholic west Belfast into Upper Ashbourne might be deplored, but it could not be resisted. One prominent activist during the evacuations said:

> The trend was clear long before 1970, and the Protestant majority in New Hull had dwindled away. This would have continued, and life would have become even more difficult for our people. The real fault lay with the sectarian allocation of houses in Kellytown to Roman Catholics. From then on Protestants could only feel at ease in Everton or Glencairn.

The removal of the religious minority from New Hull/Avoca obviously reduced the opportunity for sectarian conflict within the estates themselves. During 1971 and 1972, however, the instability in the general Upper Ashbourne area continued. During the intensified violence and enforced population movement which followed the introduction of internment in August 1971, it was one of the three most disrupted districts in Belfast. One hundred and sixty-seven families were forced to leave the area, and sixty-three families who had been intimidated from other parts of Belfast moved in (NICRC 1971, 13).

One highly unusual feature of these movements was the high proportion of private houses — seventy from the 167 — among those evacuated. All of these were in the only two small clusters of private housing in the area, Ashbourne Park and Blackwater Park, located uneasily between the increasingly segregated housing districts. In contrast to the 1970 evacuations, about seventy per cent of those departing were Catholics (NICRC 1971, 5).

Two different sets of circumstances accounted for the great majority of departures in 1971 and 1972. One was retaliatory intimidation against Catholic families in Everton/Vestry. By mid-1972 few Catholic families still lived in the estates. Retaliatory intimidation also helps to explain the removal of the small Catholic community from Blackwater, which was situated in what had become the Protestant side of Vestry Road. Apart from their attraction to stone throwers from Vestry estate, these privately owned houses were increasingly caught in a confusing welter of skirmishing between Protestant crowds, Catholic crowds and the British army. By the end of the year all had been abandoned.

The intensification of violence in the general area was the other reason for the departures from the Ashbourne estates. Since 1970 paramilitaries on both sides had become better armed, and the houses and flats alongside the Vestry Road had become an obstacle to both as they tried to get at each other. There was frequent gunfire from the heights of Vestry estate towards New Hull and Kellytown, and from those estates towards Vestry and British army patrols. Underneath the line of fire, and sometimes the object of it, was the other private housing complex, the previously secluded Ashbourne Park. By 1972 both private houses and public flats had been abandoned with varying degrees of reluctance. A swathe of territory on both sides of Vestry Road had become a devastated and unoccupied no-man's-land between an exclusively Catholic area and an exclusively Protestant one.

Over the next two years this segregation was confirmed and strengthened. On the Protestant side the evacuated Blackwater houses were reoccupied cautiously by Protestant families, although the Vestry Road flats, which were now in the front line, remained unoccupied and increasingly unoccupiable.

Paramilitary strength in New Hull/Avoca increased and the few Catholic families with relations in the security forces or police departed, hastened by an abortive bomb attack on one of them.

The presence of a guerrilla force and a conventional army in the same urban area sets up a spiral of increasing violence. The greater the paramilitary activity, the more pervasive the army's counter-guerrilla activity; the more the army leaned on the local community, the greater the civilian resentment and willingness to accept the need for paramilitary protection against army excesses. The level which anti-army feeling had reached by 1972 is demonstrated by an item from the *Tattler*, a local duplicated broadsheet:

KEEP AWAY FROM THE MILITARY
During the week a minute charge was detonated on the Cragban Road, and a British army Bomb Disposal Unit was called to deal with a suspicious parcel which had been left on the scene. An IRA sniper, who had been in position during the pre-planned incident, was unable to get a clear shot at the troops because of the people who clamoured around them. He was eventually able to wound a member of the 'DUCK SQUAD' who came along one side of the crowd. It is obvious that the military are using you and your children as shields. KEEP CLEAR.

In 1972, following 'Operation Motorman', Stanley school and Montgomery hall were occupied by the paratroop regiment as a base for rooting out the Provisional IRA from New Hull. The severity of the operation, which led to a number of arrests and internments, was described by local residents as intimidation. Certainly it encouraged families to leave the estate, and the Housing Executive had difficulty attracting families to replace them. One contemporary observation by a community worker described the danger:

I am sure that the negative aspects of the aggressive military campaign are being disastrous. Under the continual experience of apparently arbitrary harassment in home and street, family and community life is breaking down completely, and a depressing atmosphere of total despair hangs more and more heavily over the area.

(Darby and Morris 1974, 43)

Since 1975 the communities on both sides of the religious divide in Upper Ashbourne have become more preoccupied with mundane internal concerns and have grown even further apart. The hunger strikes and H-blocks issues in 1980 and 1981 provide an illustration of how final was the divorce. There was a revival of UDA activity in Everton/Vestry in anticipation of a renewal of republican violence, as there was in Suffolk and in other parts of Belfast, but it was half-hearted. In New Hull/Avoca, agitation in favour of the hunger strikers built up, but it was mainly directed against army bases. Young stone throwers confronted troops and the general rise in violence sparked off another wave of departures. One young mother whose family left New Hull at that time described the scene:

> It wasn't so much the kids from our area, but they came in from Turf Lodge and Kellytown and all over. They used to come into our garden and fling stones at the soldiers, and the soldiers fired plastic bullets back at them. It went on all night, and the Saracens [armoured cars] kept us awake.

For local residents, protesting to the rioters was as unthinkable as protesting to the army. The atmosphere of the time did not encourage qualified positions.

Despite this tension there were no serious sectarian confrontations in Upper Ashbourne. This reflected a change in how local people defined their own communities. The absolute nature of the Vestry Road 'peace line', its duration and the lack of contact between those living on either side of it had enabled each community to exclude the other from its normal considerations and concerns. Protestants in Everton/Vestry now regarded themselves as part of Protestant west Belfast, closely connected to the Shankill; for Catholics, New Hull/Avoca was the northern part of Catholic west Belfast, linked to it through Kellytown and Turf Lodge. Both were frontier areas whose cultural heartland turned them away from each other; but the confrontations often associated with frontiers were reduced by the apparently impenetrable no-man's-land between them, and by their lack of territorial ambitions against the other side. It is a paradox that the high level of cross-community conflict in 1970 demonstrated some concept of common territory, albeit one they contested. The relative calm of 1981 indicated the extent to which the concept had been lost.

Intimidation in Dunville: 1981

When did the intimidation and enforced population movements which took place in Dunville during 1981 originate? A canvass of local opinion produces as concise an answer as stabbing a finger on a line which stretched back to 1605. There is agreement, however, that there was little forewarning of the violence before 1980, and that relationships between Catholics and Protestants in the town began to deteriorate rapidly during the second half of that year when the hunger strikes campaign intensified. A rally in August 1980 ended in a riot. An attack in November on a Catholic youth by a gang called the Ranafast Young Militants, and other sectarian clashes which went through the courts, were quoted by residents as raising tension in the town. In December between 2,000 and 3,000 marchers, accompanied by tricolours, banners and five girls dressed in blankets, paraded through the town in a H-blocks protest. Loyalists complained about a 'lack of proper action by the police to deal with disruptive H-block demonstrations in the area' (*Mid-Ulster Mail*, 29 January 1981), but themselves held a 'Carson Trail' rally, complete with 3,000 loyalist marchers, Ian Paisley and six bands; the *Mail* reported that 'it was relayed by loudspeaker and could be heard over the entire town' (26 March 1981). In April 1981 one of the Catholic councillors walked out of a council meeting as a protest against 'British intransigence'. On two consecutive weeks, proposed H-block demonstrations and proposed loyalist counter-demonstrations — one organised by the Democratic Unionist Party and the other by the Orange Order — were banned under the Public Order Act. Approximately 1,200 extra police were present on both occasions. According to a local policeman, 'There were more members of the security forces than civilians in Dunville today.' In May Bobby Sands, the first hunger striker, died.

The bulk of the enforced population movement took place between May and August 1981. The increase of sectarian tension and violence during these months was not limited to Dunville. It reached a level throughout the province greater than in any period since the early 1970s.

To understand the events in Dunville it is necessary to consider the topography of those parts of the town which were most disrupted — Ranafast, the Baptistry Road estates, and Oakgrove. The interplay between these three areas accounted for most of the dynamics of the 1981 movements.

Ranafast is to the north of the town, a conservatively designed estate of mainly terraced houses where, as one tenant told a local reporter, 'the general appearance of the houses is an eyesore, lowering the tone of the estate' (*Mid-Ulster Mail*, 5 February 1981). While it was a predominantly Protestant estate in 1980 and the base of an aggressive loyalist gang known as the Ranafast Young Militants, there was a substantial Catholic minority.

The estates further to the south along the Baptistry Road — Limedrop, Clanmor and Surlead — are attractively designed, mixed modern housing, popular with tenants and still praised by tenants who fled from them in 1981. Most residents in the 175 houses were newcomers to Dunville from its hinterland and, although they were close to the Catholic church and schools, the Baptistry Road estates were religiously integrated and tranquil before 1981.

In that year Oakgrove estate, also attractively designed and popular, was still being constructed to the north-east of the town. It became the destination of many families who were intimidated from the other estates in the town.

There is little dispute that the first part of the town to be seriously affected was the Baptistry Road estates, although there is considerable disagreement about the details. On 3 May, two days before Bobby Sands' death, seventeen men, nine of them masked, were arrested for stopping traffic at the entry to the Baptistry Road estates. They had established themselves as a vigilante patrol 'to protect the estate from an attack from loyalists' — a nonexistent threat, according to the police at their trial (*Belfast Telegraph*, 15 October 1981). During the next three months a number of H-block demonstrations — usually focused on Clanmor — were held, and on occasions there were 'running battles' in the town. In July two loyalist band parades attempted

to go without permission into Cromcastle Park, a mainly
Catholic street in a mainly Protestant area, and were stopped by
rubber bullets from the police. A resulting court case showed the
extent to which an atmosphere of intimidation had grown in
Dunville: the defendant had been approached by a gang of
youths carrying sticks, following a clash between patrons of two
hotels in the south side of the town — itself an uncharacteristic
happening:

> In an effort to ascertain his religion they requested Burns to
> sing a song, but Burns refused to do so though he was of the
> same religion as the youths.
>
> (*Mid-Ulster Mail*, 13 August 1981)

In a single week at the end of August there were four riots, one
demonstration and one procession in the town. The high level of
complaints of intimidation led to the police establishing a
special intimidation squad of six detectives in Dunville at the
beginning of September.

During this period the local office of the Northern Ireland
Housing Executive was swamped with requests for transfers to
new accommodation. It was some months before the backlog, if
not the picture, had cleared. Even now it is impossible to
distinguish between normal and enforced movements, and
between those transfers which followed direct threats and
violence and those prompted by more general unease. Estimates
of the total number of enforced movements range from fifty to
120. The Housing Executive estimates that about 100 families
left their homes against their wills.

The most seriously affected areas were Clanmor and
Limedrop along the Baptistry Road. Protestant families who left
this area refer to their growing unease as H-block posters and
slogans appeared on walls and marches ended in demonstrations in the estate. There were also cases of individual intimidation, some confirmed by Catholics still living there;
threatening telephone calls, broken windows, damaged cars and
at least one petrol bomb were recalled, although direct personal
violence was uncommon. Fifteen Protestant families left the
estate in one night in May, most going to the new Oakgrove
estate and a few to stay with friends in Ranafast. The apprehensions of the remaining Protestant residents were not eased by

a meeting with unionist councillors. According to one woman who later left her home, the leader of one loyalist party on the council told them, 'There's nothing else for it. You'll have to go.' By the end of August more than thirty Protestant families had left the Baptistry Road estates, and only two remained. A few Catholic families also left during this time, some to escape the general unrest and others 'because they tried to stop the intimidation and were forced out themselves'. The view of one local policeman was that the intimidation was deliberately fomented by republican outsiders, but that the evacuations were actively encouraged by local unionist politicians. The people who left the estates at this time agree that outsiders were involved, but were sure that the leadership came from their own ex-neighbours. One woman had been greeted by 'the ringleader's wife' three years later, and replied to the greeting before she realised what she had done: 'I felt like going back to her and saying "I didn't mean to speak to you".'

During August the occasional harassment which some Catholic families in Ranafast had been experiencing since 1980 became more intense. The forms of intimidation, both general and particular, were similar to those used in Clanmor — painted slogans, marches, broken windows and telephone threats. Catholic clergy estimated that about thirty Catholic families, 'most of them old people', left Ranafast as a result of this pressure. One of them remembered the frightening atmosphere: 'Fear's an awful thing. I actually sat and shook as they shouted outside our door.' Many went to the houses which had been vacated in the Baptistry Road estates, and the Housing Executive confirms that 'a lot of them arranged straight swops'. The rural tradition of resolving sectarian housing tensions by exchanges, often arranged through the columns of the local papers, had been observed earlier in Portadown (Darby and Morris 1974, 67). Protestant families in Ranafast explain these evictions as arising from the tension of the time, saying they were an unavoidable response to the intimidation of Protestants from Clanmor. There are few denials that they were deliberate.

If there is a level of agreement about the sequence of these events, views among unionists and nationalists about the apportionment of blame for them only share a common attraction towards conspiracy theories.

For many Protestants, and for all loyalist politicians who spoke about the intimidation, the events were explained simply as an attempt by republican agitators to take over houses occupied by Protestants so that Catholics would ultimately form a majority in the town. The DUP leader in the council believed that intimidation was the result of 'two disastrous policies': the first was the containment — as distinct from confrontational — policy exercised by the police and security forces towards republican flag-flying, slogan painting and marches; the second was 'the deliberate policy of the Housing Executive to create religiously mixed estates regardless of the local context or circumstances' (*Mid-Ulster Mail*, 28 May 1981). In the single recorded acceptance by a unionist leader that there had been intimidation of Catholic families from Ranafast, the Official Unionist leader excused it as a purely retaliatory activity:

> Not one Roman Catholic would have been put out of Ranafast had the Roman Catholics not put the Protestants out of Clanmor.   (*Mid-Ulster Mail*, 12 November 1981)

The explanation of the disturbances by Catholics was similarly defensive. In his defence of the Clanmor vigilantes, their lawyer, who was also the SDLP leader in Dunville council, underlined the earlier intimidation of Catholic families and claimed that the evacuation of Clanmor was 'orchestrated' — a very familiar word from both religious groups when discussing intimidation — by the two unionist leaders in the town in an attempt to outbid each other in their struggle for leadership of the Protestant community. The objective, he argued, was to ensure that the new estate at Oakgrove became Protestant — in effect to queue-jump: 'When a new estate was built this year, it appeared there was a clear effort to establish it as a ghetto and a Protestant estate' (*Belfast Telegraph*, 15 October 1981). Although regrets were expressed for the Protestants who left Clanmor by Catholics who live there, and a number privately condemned the attacks on neighbours which took place, public acknowledgments that people had actually been intimidated were rare. According to a letter from Clanmor inhabitants headed 'Let the true facts be known' which was printed in the local paper, the evacuations were 'orchestrated by well known individuals known to the police', and the inhabitants left 'against their wishes'. Further, it was claimed that 'houses which were being vacated were systematically wrecked in the presence of certain members of the security forces' (*Mid-Ulster Mail*, 10 September 1981). Vandalism of vacated houses was less common in Dunville than in Belfast, although a local clergyman told of 'a fellow boasting to me about pulling wallpaper off walls'. The charge that off-duty members of the RUC Reserve and the security forces were involved in the intimidation was often repeated by Catholics.

For a time after September there seemed to be real danger that the process would spread to other parts of the town. Even before then, isolated families had felt forced to leave their homes in some other parts of the town. In November, however, a more serious threat appeared to be building up in Clanbeg. This sixty-six house estate, longer established and very stable, was also situated in Baptistry Road. On 26 November a letter to the *Mid-Ulster Express* from 'the only nineteen Protestants' in Clanbeg expressed their fears that the previous harmony and balance in the estate were being threatened by Protestants leaving the estate — the sort of environmental intimidation familiar in parts of Belfast. While avoiding any charges of intimidation, they called on the Housing Executive 'to put a stop to the present exchange of houses which is going on in this town'. The following issue of the paper saw three letters from Catholics in response, all sympathetic. One denied that there had been any intimidation in Clanbeg, claiming it was 'the best estate in Dunville'. A more detailed letter made four points in reply:

1. There were twenty-five, not nineteen, Protestant families in the estate.
2. Of the sixty-six houses 'forty-three were occupied by families or sons and daughters of families of mixed denomination'. (It is impossible to check this remarkable claim, but there is wide agreement from clergy and residents that the estate has a high proportion of mixed-marriage families.)
3. Catholics as well as Protestants would oppose an exchange system which threatened the balance in the estate.
4. 'We totally abhor the intimidations which took place in other estates', and suggested that a tenants' association might stabilise matters.

In the end Clanbeg survived its uneasy period and settled down again. So did Dunville.

During all this the *Mid-Ulster Express* did its desperate best to maintain a notion of balance and normality. The disturbances were covered in the paper, but usually in middle pages. 'Have CBs [citizen band radios] a Role to Play? Sectarian Barrier Breaker' was its optimistic headline on 8 January. On 14 May, less than a fortnight after Sands' death, its headline was 'Fun for all in May'. In the Police Gazette column, which was a regular section in the paper, no mention of sectarian animosity ever surfaced; the 28 May issue, at the height of the evacuations, featured a lost animal, a damaged car and a watch which had been found in the town. Only the court cases, with their constant parade of rioters, assaults and provocations, give an indication of the extent to which relationships in the town had been shaken by the events of 1981.

6.

Intimidation: The Analysis

Perceptions of Intimidation
A substantial inheritance of mythology has built up around
the process of intimidation since the first serious urban intimidation in Belfast during the early nineteenth century. Subsequent bouts of violence have refined and expanded them. It is
a mythology which sees an underlying pattern in the process,
while acknowledging that there are variations between the
experiences of people who have been intimidated.

The superficial variations are obvious. The New Hull evacuations took place at the start of the current violence and
were dramatically abrupt. In Kileen/Banduff the process went
on for some six years, lurching between periods of intense
violence and intervals of uneasy peace. Dunville's experience of
intimidation, though as abrupt as New Hull's, took place more
than a decade later and in a community which was quite unprepared for it.

Despite these differences, similar perceptions and analyses
were widely expressed in all three areas, and many of them
echoed the views of victims from earlier bouts of urban intimidation. Four were particularly common.

1. The Nostalgia Myth
This looked back on the 1960s, before the current violence
began, as a golden age when people lived together in peace and
happiness without a thought about each others' religions. It is a
paradox that those who have been intimidated from their homes
often expressed the fondest memories of past community
harmony. Old residents of Kileen recalled with pleasure the
'crack' and good company of the joint vigilante patrols of 1969.
Some Protestant and Catholic ex-neighbours from New Hull

still met in 1984 to reminisce about the old days. The common theme was loss of a sense of community, all the more valued in retrospect because of the suspicion and disharmony which had succeeded it. For some, fond memories of pre-intimidation happiness reflected dissatisfaction with their current, often unsatisfactory, conditions rather than the perfection of their previous circumstances.

2. The Vandalism Myth

In all three areas studied there were allegations that, when houses were evacuated as a result of intimidation, they were systematically vandalised. New residents found smashed toilet bowls and sinks, walls daubed with paint and graffiti; general destruction of property was reported and indeed witnessed. This was attributed to natural frustration of people who had been forced to leave their homes, and was not difficult to understand. The myth, however, was that such vindictive exhibitions were confined completely to 'the other side': 'Our people are not like that.'

3. The Invasion Myth

There was an almost universal contention that all personal acts of intimidation were carried out by outsiders to the area. Victims often recounted how local people had pleaded with them to remain, arguing that the threats had come from a few agitators from outside the district. Even in Dunville, where many of the activists were known personally to their victims, a distinction was made between old residents of the town and recent arrivals. 'It's no coincidence that the trouble started in Clanmor,' one resident pointed out. 'Sure they're not Dunville people at all.'

4. The Conspiracy Myth

It was widely believed, especially in Belfast, that intimidation — both the evacuation by one side and the arrival of the other — was highly organised and strategically motivated. There was an almost universal tendency for people to describe their condition in the terminology of military strategy. 'This is a military problem, not a sociological one', according to one community activist, and certainly it was viewed in this way by paramilitaries from both sides. Witness this description of events in Kileen in a loyalist newspaper:

> The Protestant is badly outnumbered at Kileen but as long as a call for help is sent out that call is answered. The rebels cannot be allowed to take any more Loyalist territory. New Barnsley, Moyard, Oldpark, Duncairn Gardens, must be re-taken even though no Protestant would want to live in a house once occupied by Republican scum. We must not dwell on past performances when we have beaten the rebel in every battle. We must not let the rebel bring the war to us, this must be put in reverse.   (*Ulster Loyalist*, August 1973)

The 1972 confrontation at Lucan Gardens was described by one person involved in it as 'the application of force at the weak point on the enemy's line'. In 1976, when the last Protestant families in Acre Drive were evacuated, they were told by the UDA that their position had become 'indefensible' and that there had to be a 'strategic withdrawal'. There was a good deal of preoccupation with 'holding the line' by the UDA, a concern carried to fulfilment when UDA reinforcements were brought in to defend Banduff during the Sands funeral in 1981.

This language was not confined to the activists. Ordinary people quite casually adopted similar, quite sophisticated, military terminology, and often discusssed their condition in broad strategic terms. One Protestant resident described the first Catholic families to squat in Kileen Avenue as 'hard-nosed frontier families' who had been instructed by the IRA to occupy vacated houses on the edge of Protestant Banduff in the early 1970s as a 'beachhead'. The systematic evacuations of Protestant families from Banduff in 1976 and New Hull in 1970 were seen by the evacuees as withdrawing to sounder defensive positions. There were frequent references to beachheads and footholds.

This helps to explain the importance for Banduff Protestants of maintaining a territorial link with south Belfast along White's Road, as the growth of the new Catholic estates of Poleglass and Twinbrook to their west was seen as a serious outflanking threat. Paradoxically for some Protestants, the belief that they were pawns in a broader battle plan actually provided grounds for comfort: for them the Protestant evacuations from the northern part of Montford Road were the result of an IRA plan to link Kileen to other Catholic estates to the west. Having achieved their objective, the argument went, the IRA had no further designs on Protestant Banduff.

A variant on the conspiracy myth was the belief that the construction of physical barriers between Catholic and Protestant communities arose from pressure from the army on the housing authorities to alter the physical environment in ways which made it more easily patrolled and controlled. There is a body of objective truth in these, as in all myths; houses were indeed frequently vandalised, outsiders did participate in intimidation and there were certainly instances of organised intervention by paramilitaries. As with all myths, also, these have the function of providing an acceptable interpretation of experience. For most people, they explained the horrors of intimidation and violence in a much more palatable way than the alternative view that people whom they had regarded as friends and neighbours had been responsible for evicting them. Denial of the events they had experienced, or rather of the involvement of their friends and neighbours in the events, became a talisman against their recurrence. By attributing the process to strangers — the 'invaders' who had come into the estate, or the 'other side' who vandalised houses, or paramilitary strategists with no regard for local interests — people were able to retain a memory of pre-Troubles harmony in their communities. For many the function of nostalgia was clear and explicit: it reminded them that decent behaviour between Catholics and Protestants had once been possible, and might be possible again. The intervening violence was a deviance from the earlier harmony. It is interesting, however, that religious integration was an integral part of this harmony, and that the aspiration remained as an ideal among so many people who were living in segregated communities.

Intimidation – the process

It was suggested in Chapter 4 that three main forms of intimidation may be identified from past experience. Two of them, actual physical harm and actual personal threat, were designed to create fear to the point where victims would abandon their homes. The third, environmental threat, was more closely related to anxiety about what might happen in the future.

All these forms of intimidation appeared in the three districts studied. Indeed their experiences of physical harm and personal threat were remarkably similar, including anonymous telephone calls, the sending of mass cards to Catholics, death notices in the newspapers, verbal abuse towards children, the mailing of bullets, broken windows and damage to cars. In Kileen/Banduff particularly, a number of families did experience direct violence or had been individually threatened. One family from Kileen Avenue experienced three separate gunfire attacks during which one man was seriously wounded. There were also clear cases of individuals being attacked and threatened during the Provisional IRA pressure in 1976. One ex-Banduff Protestant who moved to Ballybeen, said:

> Intimidation is not just somebody putting a gun to your back and telling you to get out, or sending you a letter, or making threats. Intimidation is a crowd of 3,000 marching past your home with hurleys or throwing a bomb into your garden or hitting your house with bullets. (*Ulster Loyalist*, August 1973)

Even in Kileen/Banduff, however, informed local opinion agreed that no more than ten per cent of the Protestant families left Kileen as a result of individual violence or threats. In Dunville the level of direct intimidation was even lower; there was certainly violence, but the availability of alternative accommodation in new estates made movement easy, and many Protestant and Catholic families simply swopped houses.

By far the most common reason for the evacuations was environmental threat; that is, not because individuals had been attacked or threatened, but because the community to which they belonged had itself become isolated and vulnerable. The spread of Catholic west Belfast during the 1970s made many Protestants feel that their community had become threatened and that the prospect of continuing to live in security at Banduff was eroding. Consequently many moved.

Some victims claimed that the process was cumulative, ascending along a scale of pressure from mild threat to actual violence. This is not supported by the experiences of intimidated families. In Dunville and Banduff, for example, many forms of threat were used simultaneously and the process was too spontaneous to allow such calculated escalation.

All three districts experienced the third category of intimidation — perceived environmental threat. People who had been intimidated often saw themselves as helpless pawns in a paramilitary chess game. Local Protestant and Catholic communities in Belfast were viewed as organisms, advancing and retreating, colonising and infiltrating. People talked of the need to 'hold the line' or to 'retreat to a defensible position'; the other side had to be prevented from 'getting a foot in'. In Dunville too local politicians watched every advance and retreat of the sectarian boundaries closely, and the debate in the local newspaper about the possible advance of Catholic territory into Clanbeg was conducted with detailed familiarity of the religion of every resident in the district. In all three districts people analysed demographic trends in minute detail. A general perception that 'the other side' was becoming dominant could convert a trickle of departures into a flood.

It is not possible to estimate with any precision the proportion of people who moved as a result of being threatened, and the proportion who left to avoid living in what was becoming an increasingly alien environment. Indeed it is often difficult to distinguish between the two. In Old Banduff, for example, direct violence was used to expel Catholic families who had moved across the Montford Road in 1976, but it arose directly from fear that the Catholics would establish what the Protestants considered a 'beachhead' in Protestant territory. In Dunville the first Catholics left Ranafast because of direct threat, but their departure isolated other families who had not experienced direct threat or violence and led in turn to their leaving. While motives for movement were similarly confused in all areas, a minority of evacuees had themselves experienced direct violence or threat, although most could quote cases where it had happened. Expectation of trouble in the future was a much more powerful determinant of flight than experience of violence in the past. Most people had moved due to an anticipation of violence, rather than as a reaction to it.

In Belfast this applied particularly to Protestant evacuees. Although almost all evacuees believed that they were victims of general demographic patterns beyond their control, Protestant minorities were much more likely to depart as a result of them. In both New Hull in 1970 and Banduff in 1976 the departures of the last Protestant families were organised by local politicians or paramilitaries; even in Dunville some local politicians encouraged Protestant families to leave Clanmor in 1981. In none of the three areas was the departure of Catholic families organised in the same way, although the confrontations in Kileen after 1972 were stimulated and supported by the Provisional IRA. Catholics, on the other hand, more frequently mentioned threats of actual violence as the reasons for their departure.

The explanation of the differences between Catholic and Protestant movements in Belfast was directly related to the city's demographic structure. In 1969 about twenty-six per cent of Belfast's population was Catholic, and eighty-one per cent of them lived in the Falls and Ardoyne districts. In those districts they formed very large local majorities (Poole and Boal 1973, 14). The rest of the city was largely composed of predominantly Protestant communities with Catholic minorities. Consequently, when the large population shifts began later that year the two religious groups were affected in quite different ways. The general pattern of enforced population movement among Catholics was a transfer from communities where they formed minorities into Catholic west Belfast (NICRC 1971). For Protestants much of the movement came from communities threatened by the resulting expansion of Catholic west Belfast. So, although both groups experienced the full range of intimidation, Catholics more often left their homes as a consequence of direct intimidation, and Protestant movements were more often an attempt to avoid violence in the future. Catholic evacuees were more likely to be isolated minority families; Protestant evacuees were more likely to be isolated minority communities.

The two types of movement were closely interwoven, for there was a high level of reciprocity in the process. The process itself might be regarded as a circle of intimidation.

Like all circles, the starting point is arbitrary. For many Protestant communities in the city the initial first-hand experience of community violence was the arrival of Protestant evacuees from other parts of Belfast. Their presence often led to the first expressions of resentment towards Catholics living in the area. Catholic families, already apprehensive, described this period as one of growing isolation and vulnerability. Some were threatened and a few were attacked. Many considered moving for the first time. Even if they decided to stay, others in the area probably left, emphasising the earlier isolation. The great majority of the Catholic evacuees sought refuge in Catholic west Belfast, which was already overcrowded. New estates which had just been completed or were still being built, like Kileen and Twinbrook, became predominantly Catholic. This expansion of the Catholic heartlands accounted for much of the Protestant evacuations over the next few years. Protestants feared that vacated houses in places like Banduff and New Hull would increasingly be occupied by Catholic families and that their community would be surrounded by Catholic communities. In addition to actual cases of direct threat or violence, the newcomers were seen as a beachhead for Catholic expansion into previously unthreatened Protestant communities. Individuals began to leave. Others became nervous. Their arrival into predominantly Protestant communities in other parts of the city completed the circle, and often started a new one.

Thus each movement created pressure in its reception area, pressure which often led to intimidation for a family there. And so it went on. The process was dynamic and tended to escalate.

While the circle was distinctive to developments in the greater Belfast area between 1969 and 1975, all communities affected by intimidation experienced a similar progression in their patterns of evacuation. This progression followed two parallel lines — one relating to social class and the other to sectarianism.

The manner in which each local community was affected by intimidation was closely related to its social composition. Many minority families who wished to flee from intimidation were unable to do so: the cost of transport or of renting private houses was too high, and rent arrears excluded some from applying to the housing authorities for transfers. The result was that the early evacuees were often the families with higher incomes and records of regular rent payments. These families often provided a high proportion of local leaders — the ones 'best equipped to hold the place together and provide leadership', as a Banduff resident put it. Left behind were those who had been locked into an unpleasant environment by their deprivation — the poor, the old and single-parent families.

The relationship between the sectarian structure of each community and the intimidation of minority members was even closer. The process took place in a number of stages. First was a sorting out of any mixed region between the two religious communities, creating a recognisable boundary between them. In Kileen/Banduff this was the Montford Road and the tall fences erected to protect Old Banduff; in Upper Ashbourne it was the empty and demolished houses along Vestry Road. The next stage was the departure of the minority families who remained on the wrong side of the boundary, so that it came to mark the limits of two exclusive communities. In some districts the process continued beyond these stages, with the eviction of political and other non-conformists — Catholics and Protestants who opposed the paramilitaries from their own community, and, in some cases, even individuals who offended community moral standards by sexual promiscuity, drug taking or general crime. The attempts of the Provisional IRA to discipline the 'hoods' in Kileen proceeded from the same search for security which had forced Protestant families to leave the estate in 1972, and which only came from living among 'your own sort'.

It is possible to view the intimidation process from two major perspectives. One emphasises the activities of the intimidators, and regards it as an aggressive and sometimes a conspiratorial phenomenon. Communities are viewed as sectarian organisms, and the periodic outbreaks of intimidation since the 1830s as purgatives — the expulsion of foreign elements from the communal body through spasms of purifying zeal.

The other view stresses the perceptions and reactions of the victims. The population movements are explained as a simple flight from violence and fear and a search for security.

The two views overlap. Families forced to flee from their homes into a new community may be prepared to condone the use of force to maintain its ethnic 'purity'. But the process is essentially defensive. The common motive is a search for security. People left their homes because they no longer felt safe, and sought an area where they did. In a context of community violence, safety was defined as living among one's own group, and the fewer neighbours from the other group, the better. This often meant that both Catholics and Protestants sought the comfort of a ghetto. Its attraction was that it provided a defensible community — an estate like Old Banduff or an area like Catholic west Belfast — where a local minority became a majority. Within such ghettos there was an agreed need to exclude members of the other group.

Stabilising and threatening factors

But most people in Northern Ireland do not live in ghettos, nor was intimidation a universal or a permanent process. Few communities in Northern Ireland were affected seriously by it. In most rural communities, for example, sectarian tensions remained low or were peacefully resolved by arranging house exchanges, as happened in Dungannon in the early 1970s (Darby and Morris, 1974). Many middle class districts in Belfast itself experienced no disturbances even during August 1969 and August 1971, when the city experienced its most serious intimidation. Even in those districts which did, overt intimidation was absent for substantial periods.

The three districts examined in this research all experienced intimidation, but the duration, forms and intensity varied greatly. The variety was partly a consequence of different external pressures on each community, but was also influenced by their peculiar internal structures. Among the most important variables which determined whether, when or how a community was affected by intimidation were public agencies, community initiatives and paramilitary organisations.

1. Agency roles: the housing authorities and the security forces

In all three districts intimidation was confined almost entirely to public rather than private housing, and in all three the first consequence was that the housing authorities lost control over housing allocation. In Dunville some months had passed before the Housing Executive was able to regain control. In Kileen, on the other hand, the executive tried to adopt a more interventionist approach. They refused to allocate houses vacated by Protestants to Catholic families in 1972 and, backed by the army, delayed the collapse of the Protestant community in Acre

Drive. But they could not prevent it. The Housing Executive had the authority to prevent official transfers of tenancies, but could do nothing to stop squatting — ultimately having to recognise the reality and confirm tenancies. However this did not mean that the executive was powerless in affecting the rate of population change in the area. It may not have been able to prevent the occupation of vacant houses, but it could and did make it difficult for Protestant families to transfer officially to other parts of the city. When Protestant Banduff had shrunk in 1975 to the boundaries which it still held nine years later, the executive's policy was to deny all transfer requests. This policy created bitter resentment among Protestants at the time, but in 1984 most agreed that the executive's obduracy during the nervous months of 1975 and 1976 was responsible for the continuing existence of Protestant Banduff as a community.

The influence of Housing Executive policy on the number of evacuations was considerable, even in apparently innocuous ways. The determination of tenants to leave an estate was influenced by its condition as well as by the level of intimidation. The high number of squatters in Lower Kileen encouraged departures, as did the widespread local belief that Avoca and Old Banduff were being used by the Housing Executive as 'dumping grounds' for deprived families. The subsequent reduction of squatting, from 4,500 acknowledged cases in 1973 to 797 in 1983, helped to stabilise communities and reduce the number of population movements. But the belief that some estates were 'dumping grounds' continued to encourage demographic instability.

An equally destabilising factor was the apparent contradictions in the executive's policy on sectarian allocation. The official line was that the executive's job was housing people where they wanted to be housed rather than social engineering. In some instances it was criticised for this policy, which led to the disappearance of minority populations from Twinbrook and other districts. On other occasions, however, the executive refused to allow transfers from Kileen and Old Banduff, because they wished to 'hold the community together' — indeed it is acknowledged by both local and central officials that it was 'official policy' to hold Old Banduff together. The confusion arose because such decisions were taken by district managers rather than centrally, the key question about any transfer being 'Is it possible to find a new tenant?' The confusion about the executive's policy on allocation arose from the fact that it did not have one.

The movements from New Hull in 1970 and from Dunville in 1981 were rapid and unexpected, and the police and army had little influence on events. In 1972, however, the army set out to resist the southwards expansion of Catholic Kileen, first by establishing an army post and later by attempting to hold a 'peace line'. Neither was successful, except in briefly delaying the advance. However, a number of the remaining Protestant residents in Old Banduff emphasised the critical role of the Carrytree army/police post in maintaining the sectarian boundary along the Montford Road between 1975 and 1984. They also claimed that any relaxation of security vigilance would threaten the future of their community. The latter estimation is more convincing than the former. The absence of security forces may facilitate intimidation; but their presence does not necessarily prevent it.

2. Local initiatives

There was no shortage of local effort to resist intimidation and maintain communities in which both Catholics and Protestants could live together. More than 1,000 vigilantes patrolled the North Ashbourne estates under the Ashbourne Joint Committee in 1969, and Catholics and Protestants also formed joint patrols in Banduff. However by 1972 the camaraderie of those days had dissipated and the remaining defence groups had become sectarian. The intimidation in Dunville was so unexpected that no preliminary steps had been taken to anticipate it. Here too, however, it was also condemned by most community leaders, although there was considerable sectarian disagreement about where responsibility lay.

The growth of a feeling of territorial inevitability in the Belfast communities was a major obstacle to holding together a mixed-religion community. Nevertheless there was consider-able support for such an ideal, particularly in Kileen/Banduff: in 1969 there was co-ordination between vigilante patrols in the area; and there were at least three attempts to hold a peace line. All these initiatives received considerable backing from army and police and even became enshrined in the Housing Executive's allocation policies. But none of them was successful in preventing the erosion of Protestant Banduff. Indeed the area's longest period of stability had been that which followed the highly segregated post-1976 arrangements, divided by physical barriers. This may suggest that attempts to preserve an integrated community during periods of violence are unlikely to succeed. It also suggests that, after a period of enforced separation, people were only prepared to restore relationships when their most serious apprehensions had been eased. One Protestant, forced to move from Banduff to Cregagh, said that, although he was prepared to work and drink with Catholics, he was not prepared to live among them.

Apart from the *ad hoc* vigilante groups which were established as a reaction to violence, few of the more conventional organisations in the community had much success in resisting the spread of intimidation. The growth of community action in Belfast did not take place until the 1970s, so Banduff and the Upper Ashbourne lacked the infrastructure of community groups which might have contributed to stability. However, they did not lack churches. Church halls and schools were converted into relief centres; food and shelter were provided; arrangements were made for the transfer of children to new schools and families to new parishes. But none of the people interviewed mentioned clergymen providing a lead in resisting the process. In all three districts the clergy concentrated on providing relief rather than leadership, and settled for dealing with the effects of intimidation rather than preventing its spread. Some Catholic clergy justified this role by referring to the church's historical inability to appeal effectively against militant nationalism; one, while opposing violence, admitted some sympathy for its causes. In the Presbyterian church, ministers revealed an awareness of the fate of clergymen whose views moved too far from those of their congregations. One minister in Dunville provided an explanation for his own help-lessness during the intimidation of 1981: he claimed that, while his influence was considerable in normal circumstances, his views were simply ignored in the violent and inflamed atmosphere of the hunger strikes and intimidation.

The failure of moderate community leaders — clergy,

teachers, community activists — to provide reassurance and direction at critical times during the intimidation process was widely criticised. Thirteen years later people who were forced to leave New Hull still resented the way in which their future was decided by politicians from outside the estate, and blamed it partly on the weakness of their own leaders. Community activists often accepted the charge. Their problem was a familiar one for leaders whose positions rely on personal popularity rather than official status. During periods of intense sectarian violence and fear, to urge moderation may attract accusations of weakness or even treachery and may undermine the leader's position. Those who attempted to provide a lead by condemning intimidation and violence often found themselves without followers. For some the loss of their credibility seemed too high a price to pay for resisting developments which, however distasteful, seemed to be inevitable anyway. The views of the Dunville clergyman found echoes among leaders of moderate opinion in all districts which experienced intimidation. In times of high violence, people looked for direction to violent leaders. Moderate politicians, clergymen and community leaders became, temporarily but literally, redundant.

3. Paramilitaries

At first sight the paramilitaries who might have been expected to benefit from this trend appear to have maintained a low profile during the actual periods of intimidation. In Dunville neither republican nor loyalist paramilitaries were directly involved as organisations in intimidation, although individual members were. Even in Belfast, direct intervention was rare and occasional. Certainly the Provisional IRA was involved in the confrontation along Kileen Avenue in 1972, and the UDA evacuated Protestant families from Acre Drive and intimidated Catholic families from 'the wrong side' of Montford Road in 1975. Paramilitary organisations were more visibly active in maintaining internal control than in imposing it on their opponents. In the main there is little evidence of a consistent paramilitary involvement in direct organised intimidation.

This arose, not from the paramilitaries' lack of interest in developments, but from their knowledge that direct involvement was rarely needed. Almost exactly a century before, Sir James Stephen had observed how rarely underground movements needed to use intimidation when their objectives were close to those of their constituency:

> A relatively small amount of shooting in the legs will effectively deter an immense mass of people from paying rents which they do not want to pay.   (Stephen 1886, 773)

In Belfast during the 1970s there was a similar relationship between force and general wishes. The movement of both religious groups into segregated quarters was fuelled by fear and was often accepted and approved by the paramilitaries. Their role was to intervene only when the process was threatening their interests — to apply the fine tuning rather than to change the channel. 'We had very little to do with it,' according to one local paramilitary. 'The people needed houses and took them.' The clash along Kileen Avenue was a rare example of paramilitary confrontation, where both groups decided to make a stand. More characteristic was the decision by the UDA to evacuate the remaining Protestants from Acre Drive to a more easily defended position south of the Montford Road. The relative infrequency of this sort of selective intervention merely underlined the watching nature of the brief which the paramilitaries had adopted.

Northern Ireland: an intimidatory culture

During periods of sectarian violence, publicity and public interest have concentrated on cases in which individuals were directly threatened and forced to leave their homes. The report on the 1857 riots in Belfast, for example, highlighted the fact that the first three victims were mixed-marriage families, and much newspaper coverage of the intimidation during the 1970s also concentrated on individual cases of direct violence. These were certainly dramatic but, as they were often regarded as atypical and abberant, they encouraged a general underestimate of the prevalence of intimidation. In practice this form of individual intimidation accounted for only a small proportion of the families who were forced to leave their homes. While it is impossible to be precise, the experiences of the victims, and assessments by community leaders and the police, suggest that it accounted for about twelve per cent of families who moved in Kileen/Banduff, and less than ten per cent in both North Ashbourne and Dunville, and that only a small proportion of these were directly carried out by paramilitary organisations. Most people who left their homes had not been singled out for violence.

The more subtle mechanisms which account for the great majority of movements arise from Northern Ireland's culture. There are two components in the intimidation process — the threats or actions of the intimidator and the perception of the victim. People born in Northern Ireland become conscious from an early age of the sectarian divisions in society; according to Cairns, children are aware of the Protestant-Catholic split from the age of eleven (Cairns 1980). They soon become sensitive to social nuances and taboos which are not always apparent to outsiders. As a result they may not apply for jobs in certain factories, or discuss controversial subjects in certain settings, or live in particular districts. They know that, in some circumstances, outsiders may wish to dispossess or evict them simply for belonging to their own community, and that indiscretions within that community may also be punished. Theirs is an intimidatory culture, and they know the limits of behaviour permissible within it.

The rules which regulate relationships operate even in periods when there is little overt violence. Rosemary Harris showed that an awareness of sectarian division was central even in a small rural community during the 1950s (Harris 1972). During periods of intense violence and enforced population movement, fear and the search for security make observation of the rules more crucial.

Those who are prepared to use violence are as aware of the rules as their victims, and can use them to advantage. There is ample evidence in Northern Ireland that threats, direct or implied, have often been carried out. Consequently direct intimidation, though used, was often unnecessary. As rumours and experiences of violence became more common, people felt more vulnerable to threats, real and imagined. The violence had created a culture of intimidation, which was more subtle and invidious than cruder forms of intimidation. This itself became the main agent of intimidation and, even when not supplemented by threats, led to the evacuations of entire communities in the city.

Many victims of intimidation naturally viewed it as an aggressive process, and some of them believed that it was deliberately turned on and off by paramilitary organisations. In reality the power of intimidation springs from its essentially defensive nature. Local minorities were driven by violence and fear to move to other communities in which they could become part of a majority. They were often willing to encourage the expulsion of ethnic opponents from their new community. The intensity of the search for security provides a more satisfactory explanation of the population changes of the early 1970s than paramilitary pressure.

7.

Relationships in the Communities

COLEMAN described the relationships between combatants as 'the chains which carry controversy from beginning to end as long as they remain unbroken, but which also provide the means of softening the conflict if means can be found to break them' (Coleman 1971, 256). Local communities affected by intimidation and population movements are in the vanguard of the conflict, having suffered more than most. This chapter examines the ways in which relationships have developed, both between the two groups and within them, in the years after the three communities had experienced their worst violence.

Kileen/Banduff

Relations between Catholics and Protestants

There was no questioning the reality of the division between Kileen and Banduff. The existence of two distinct communities was widely acknowledged on both sides, and was confirmed by the shifting nomenclatures in the area. Although 'Banduff' was commonly used to describe the streets north of Montford Road in the early 1970s, few of the Catholics living there used the term naturally. 'We might say we were from Banduff if we were stopped by the Brits. They might think we were Prods and let us away quickly,' as one resident put it. By 1983 the most common name for the Catholic part of the estate had become Kileen, and there was some degree of loyalty to it. For example, locals were in no doubt that it was quite distinct from the neighbouring private housing estates of Montford and Hillhead, and from Glencollin to the north which had been built during the 1970s. 'All the area from the Hollow Road to Montford Road is Kileen Estate. That's what it's called,' one local said. 'It's never called Banduff, except to impress people from posh estates like Montford.'

Personal friendships or visits between the residents of Banduff and Kileen were rare. 'They have nothing to fear from us,' according to one Catholic; 'we have no contact with them.' Among the local leaders of the two communities there was often a vague sympathy for the notion of improving relationships within the broader area, and Catholics had contributed a substantial sum towards the renovation of the local Church of Ireland church when it was damaged by a bomb. Nevertheless community leaders were also aware of how leaders from other parts of the city had fallen from grace by embracing cross-religious contacts without the support of their followers. 'You can't push things too quickly here,' in the words of one local leader. 'Suspicions are still too strong.' So, despite the existence of a Protestant and Catholic Encounter group (PACE) in the area, its membership was small and its activities circumspect almost to the point of inertia. Joint holidays to America in 1982 and Christmas parties for pensioners were the main forms of cross-religion socialising.

The existence of facilities along the Montford and Banduff roads provided some occasions for contact between Catholics and Protestants. In 1983 the Housing Executive claimed that their sub-office and the Citizens' Advice Bureau on the Protestant side of Montford Road was used by 'both sides of the community' (Northern Ireland Housing Executive 1983). Weekly coffee mornings in the Methodist church and a Catholic-organised thrift shop in Banduff Road attracted custom from both communities. However, although both groups freely used the main shops there, Protestants were reluctant to use another butchery and general shop no less than 200 yards to the east, and Catholics less inclined to shop at the co-op a similar distance to the west. There was no possibility of Protestants being willing to attend the large new leisure centre at Andersonstown, and some resentment that their geographical proximity was used as an argument by the authorities against a similar provision nearer Banduff. Although Protestants were willing to cross Montford Road to visit the chip shop on Banduff Road, they regarded as 'hostile territory' the library and day centre beside the Methodist church which, to the untrained and even the trained eye, appeared to be in a much more neutral area. Equally surprising, perhaps, was the willingness of Protestants to use public transport and the 'people's taxis', which were regarded by many as a republican front; both buses and taxis followed routes through republican areas, but the lack of a good alternative service may provide part of the answer.

Just as complex are the distinctions between acceptable and unacceptable forms of institutional contact. One community centre in Kileen was prepared to welcome old age pensioners' lunch clubs from Banduff,, which had no centre of its own, but it rejected a request to hold prayer meetings there. 'None of us are very good Catholics, but we don't like prayer meetings,' said one regular attender. Shamrock Community Workshop, on the other hand, although established on the Catholic side of the estate, was rigorously controlled from the start by a committee from both the Catholic and Protestant communities. Indeed its management claimed that Protestants were slightly over-represented among the eighty-plus young people there, in relation to their share of the population. Political discussion is forbidden, and more pride is taken in the fact that the workshop's football team was integrated than in its results. The Workshop was considering using two of the houses on the Protestant side of Montford Road as a 'drop-in' centre for the youth of the area which would have given it a presence on both sides of the road.

Relationships between the schools provide the best illustration of the delicate judgments exercised in cross-religious contacts. Although the two primary schools which served the majority of Protestant and Catholic children on the estate had little contact with each other, there was a level of co-operation between the Protestant Banduff primary school and another neighbouring Catholic primary school. This took the form of football matches, carol singing and even curricular co-operation. So amiable was the relationship that the Catholic principal suggested that Banduff children might use a swimming pool in his area. 'I thought long and hard about it,' said the Banduff principal, conscious of the possible reaction from some parents, 'and decided to reject the offer.'

So the pattern of contact was highly functional. Where there was a clear material advantage in co-operation, people were quite prepared to mix. So the inconvenience of finding alternative shopping or transport arrangements overcame instinctive suspicions, and Protestants were prepared to send their children to Shamrock Community Workshop, despite its being in a Catholic locality, because training was highly prized in an area of high unemployment. When the point of contact was regarded as a luxury rather than a necessity, such as the library or swimming pool, it was much more infrequent. Hence there was a confusing mixture of functional co-operation and voluntary segregation.

The confusion was a result of both the sectarian strife of the early 1970s and the easing of tensions since 1976. Some of the co-operative initiatives arose from a general wish to improve community relations. Others, especially on the Protestant side, were motivated by a desire to hold their own community together. Nevertheless there were still fears on the Protestant side, and a growing preoccupation with its own internal affairs on the Catholic side of the community. The result has been the emergence of cautious contact in certain activities, but the maintenance of an essential polarisation.

Inside Protestant Banduff: Internal Relationships

Within this polarisation were two distinctly organised communities. Of these the less complex, at least in terms of public activities, was Banduff, the small Protestant enclave to the south of Montford Road. It was screened from the neighbouring Catholic estates to its south and east by tall, corrugated tin fences. Similar fences along the Montford Road divided it from Kileen; this helped to create a fortress-like atmosphere and, a local policeman suggested, an introverted community.

The allocation policy adopted by the Housing Executive was a matter of major importance for Banduff's residents. It was acknowledged, sometimes with resentment, that the Housing Executive's refusal to allow any transfers from the estate during its period of greatest threat in 1976 and 1977 was probably the main reason why further mass evacuations had not taken place. The housing authority confirmed that it had indeed adopted such a practice and was still treating requests for transfers with caution seven years later. As late as 1984 the mother of a policeman, whose son was unable to visit her for security reasons, had been refused a transfer and was contemplating going to law. Some residents believed that the Housing Executive, in its attempts to fill vacancies as soon as possible, was too ready to admit what were often referred to as 'problem families' — single-parent families, prisoners, the poor and the unemployed. 'It has become a dumping ground for Prods in Belfast,' in the view of one older resident. The executive, while refuting the charge of 'dumping', conceded that the estate had a disproportionately high number of single-parent households and much petty crime. The general poverty of Banduff, even among the employed, was testified by the fact that more than half the children in Banduff primary school qualified for free school meals on the basis of low parental income. To the remaining group of longer-term residents, it seemed that the stable elements in Banduff have been moving out and replaced by a transient population.

The longer-term residents were more likely to be employed, to live in the estate's better housing and to support community initiatives. The most active period for such initiatives was that following the Acre Drive evacuations in 1976-7. At that time a popular and energetic Methodist minister encouraged the formation of Banduff Community Association, and a programme of activities was started. Some locals have fond memories of these years, when there was a 'great community spirit' and considerable commitment to holding the area together. There was also a higher level of cross-religious contact with Kileen in 1977, when old people from Banduff visited Acre Drive community centre, than in 1984. The decline in this type of initiative appeared to be more closely related to the departure of particular community leaders than to any general factor.

The enthusiasm of 1977 had largely dissipated by 1984. By that time some of the local residents were unaware that Banduff Community Association was still in existence, despite its having a house in the estate, and others described it as moribund. Organised activity in general was low. Despite attempts to revive community spirit in 1982, when the Housing Executive, the community association, a local minister and some others began to meet, the executive's view was that 'the apathetic attitude of many residents has made it difficult for the community association to get the level of support they need to be effective' (Northern Ireland Housing Executive 1983). The effort was abandoned from fear of a paramilitary takeover.

Even the UDA, although quite strong in neighbouring areas, was weak in Banduff and not well regarded. 'They're not called the Wombles for nothing,' was the view of one local leader, a reference to their incompetence. Most people acknowledged, however, that the strength and level of activity of paramilitary organisations was variable, not constant. Much depended on the quality of local leadership, which changed frequently in Banduff during the 1970s. Older residents sometimes made a distinction between those elements within the UDA which were interested in political and community action and the elements they described as 'the cowboys' — the physical force side of the organisation which could terrorise the estate with its hoodlum activities. In Banduff the strength of the UDA had been weak since the late 1970s and its interest spasmodic. Nevertheless, during the Bobby Sands funeral in 1981, which was diverted from processing along the Montford Road, popular local belief had it that more than 300 UDA men from all parts of the city and even from Scotland were inside Banduff, ready to defend it against invasion. If there is any basis for the belief, it demonstrates the irregular nature of UDA interest in the affairs of Banduff.

Since 1972 there had been a number of attempts to stage a campaign for the building of a community centre in Banduff. In that year a survey by the now defunct Old Banduff Residents' Association claimed that seventy-four per cent of the residents wanted a centre. The subsequent campaign, and at least two later attempts to acquire premises for a youth clubhouse or community centre, had foundered in the face of general apathy and internal rivalries among the activists. In 1984 the only effective organised local activities — a youth club, uniformed youth organisations like the Boys' Brigade and the Girl Guides who moved their meetings from the Presbyterian church because of harassment, and bingo evenings — were taking place in Banduff primary school and were not well supported. The Parent-Teachers' Association, for example, was rarely able to muster more than ten parents, although the principal had no difficulty finding volunteers for driving minibuses and fund raising.

So there was little evidence of dynamism or community

commitment in Banduff in 1984 and factional differences were an obstacle to changing the situation. However kinship ties, which were still close among the older residents, were a stabilising factor, persuading some Banduff families to remain in the area despite the general uneasiness. Indeed the housing authorities noticed that some young couples had begun to move into Banduff since 1980, most of them relatives and friends of existing tenants. Nevertheless, as a social worker said, 'The area is very depressed and passive and does not push for amenities.'

Inside Catholic Kileen: Internal Relationships

The high level of community activity in Catholic Kileen, north of Montford Road, contrasted with its absence in old Banduff. In 1983 more than forty groups were active in the estate, engaged in activities ranging from bingo to political activism.

One of the most striking of these interests has been the revival of Irish language and culture since 1980. In common with other republican areas of Belfast, this revival was demonstrated in Kileen by the proliferation of wall paintings and slogans. It was claimed by some that the Gaelic tradition in Belfast had a long and unbroken provenance, and that this had merely taken on a modern mode by the arrival during the 1970s of a community of Irish-speaking families and an Irish language school in nearby Bernards Road. Certainly the *Bunscoil*, as it was known, was an important focus for language enthusiasts and its roll included several children from Kileen, with more on the waiting list. The post-1980 revival, however, seemed to be connected more closely to republican prisoners returning home after an incarceration during which many had attended Irish language classes, and encouraging its spread as a manifestation of republicanism and patriotism. It was also noticeable that the Irish revival emerged in the years following the worst violence in the area rather than during the periods of violence themselves. So it may represent a more tranquil, post-revolutionary form of community identification.

The community's identity was also expressed in the groups — many of them small — which operated in the estate. Most of these clustered around four main axes, although there was considerable overlap between them and occasional sharp conflict. These were: 1. Sporting Groups; 2. Political and

Paramilitary Groups; 3. the Catholic Church; and 4. Community Action.

1. Sporting Groups

The high level of sporting activity in the area was partly the effect of a Gaelic football complex beside Kileen, containing three football fields and four Gaelic Athletic Association (GAA) club houses. The clubs drew membership from a wide geographical segment of west Belfast and, apart from their common interest in sport, varied somewhat in their activities. Some were active in encouraging cultural events and had Irish music and dancing sessions. One was described by locals as a 'drinking den'.

Although the clubs provided bases for a range of activities much wider than sports, they had little involvement with community activities in Kileen and avoided the adoption of political stances except in exceptional circumstances. They earned the approval of some parents for offering a healthy outlet for their children. 'They do not get enough credit,' according to a local priest. Occasionally they have attracted scorn from local republicans for their political caution, and some general disapproval for encouraging drinking in the club houses.

2. Political and Paramilitary Groups

'Lower Kileen supports the Provisionals', accordingly to the gable messages in the estate, but 'the war' has rarely been in evidence within the estate since the mid-1970s. On the other hand the paramilitaries had assumed a growing role in policing the district. In 1977, for example, a formal statement published by the Belfast Brigade showed how seriously the IRA took its claims to enforce law and order:

> In recent weeks a series of robberies have taken place in the Nationalist Ghetto areas of Belfast; those robbed have ranged from social clubs to milkmen and in most cases they have been robbed by a local gangster element using the name of the Republican army. Our volunteers were not involved in these acts. Indeed it is our policy not to involve ourselves in this type of action. The Belfast Brigade would like to warn that

anyone caught using the name of the Irish Republican Army in these circumstances will be executed.

(*Andersonstown News*, 10 December 1977)

There were deep divisions within the community about the involvement of paramilitaries in such a policing role. These came to a head in the 1980s when the IRA carried out a number of sanctions against petty criminals, and especially the 'hoods', who stole cars and drove them through the area to general disapproval. The divisions within Kileen about how joyriding should be tackled were well illustrated during a public meeting on the subject held in 1984. One speaker stated that 'it was the duty of the IRA to be the law in the area'; another responded, 'some fucking Christian you are'; the father of a teenager who had been beaten up by the IRA also protested and left the meeting; a man whose house had been invaded by an out-of-control car put another view. Eventually a vigilante patrol was formed, and soon it was accused of waging personal vendettas against young people (Mullan, 21 January 1985). The estate was deeply riven by the issue, and neither the police nor the paramilitaries had an unchallenged mandate to provide law and order.

There were no divisions about Kileen's political sympathies; the estate was overwhelmingly republican. In the words of one activist, 'the strengths may vary, but they're all republican'. During another conversation with a Sinn Fein canvasser during the 1983 Westminster election, she summed up Kileen's political affiliations thus: 'About thirty per cent don't care, but fifty per cent or so will vote Sinn Fein.' 'What about the SDLP?' she was asked. 'They have very little support.' 'Alliance?' She laughed, obviously at the naïveté of the question.

The graffiti confirmed her diagnosis. Apart from the prevalence of republican acronyms, some messages were clearly directed, by their sentiments and their positioning at eye level, towards patrolling British soldiers, like this one, skilfully painted on the end wall of a flat:

When you came to this land
You said you came to understand.
Soldier we're tired of your understanding.
Tired of the knock upon the door.

> Tired of the rifle-butt on the head.
> Tired of the jails and the beatings.
> Tired of the deaths of old friends.
> Tired of the tears and funerals —
>   those endless endless funerals.
> Is this your understanding?

Republicanism was the main theme, therefore, although one message which appeared in 1983 proclaimed a more cosmopolitan cause:

> The worker is the slave of capitalist society.
> The female worker is the slave of that slave.

A recent development, in Kileen and in other parts of Belfast, has been the entry of Sinn Fein into community politics. This dated from the period of high tension of the 1981 hunger strikes during which a Kileen man was among the strikers. The Hollow Community Centre in Kileen was twice taken over by the Provisionals as a 'field hospital', in anticipation of a period of intense violence and the workers were forced to leave. Since then Provisional Sinn Fein had been more active on local issues, encouraging a welfare rights survey in the estate and taking over the management of the Middle Kileen Residents' Association. The subsequent collapse of that body was attributed by some local community workers to Sinn Fein's obsession with constitutional rather than local issues and its lack of professionalism. 'They were not able to sustain a group; they refer welfare cases to their Falls Road Incident Centre,' according to a community worker, implying that this was an inappropriate way to resolve the problems.

The alarm about the politicisation of community work by the intervention of Sinn Fein was not peculiar to Kileen and some community activists feared that it would lead to the collapse of other groups. On the other hand some social workers in the area have praised Sinn Fein's work in the communities, one saying, 'they are very active and often constructive; their referrals are usually sensible, not aggressive'. Others too, who opposed IRA violence, believed that Sinn Fein's new community involvement had 'opened more constructive avenues' for republican supporters. In 1984 the clash of interests with community

workers was a symptom of a potential future conflict rather than
a serious current reality.

3. The Catholic Church

The usual religious groups associated with the Catholic church
in Ireland were also present in Kileen. A group described
vaguely as 'the charismatics' by the parish priest had been
formed, and the St Vincent de Paul society had played an
important relief role during the population movements of the
early 1970s. Since the late 1970s the church had become
increasingly active in the creation and sponsoring of what might
be described as social groups. These included the Cosmos youth
club, a senior citizens' committee, a communications group
which produced a newsletter and an environmental group
whose apparently innocuous aim of improving the appearance
of the parish had political implications. In addition the church
was a prime mover in establishing the Shamrock Community
Workshop and in attracting positions for about forty PACE
workers.

These interventions were primarily due to the personalities
and philosophy of the clergymen in the parish during this
period, who placed great emphasis on the need for strong leadership in the estate. 'The parish is the natural unit in this
community,' is the view of one; 'if it is not active, the void will be
filled by paramilitaries and radicals.' This view of the church as
the driving force in educational, economic, political, social and
security matters provided the rationale for a strong campaign
against the Provisionals, which was conducted with the style
and vigour of the counter-reformation. The most obvious arena
for confrontation was the issue of graffiti in the estate. The presence of dark brown paint on gable walls proclaimed the zeal and
painting ability of the church's environmental group which had
been trying to remove the political slogans. The ebb and flow
of this struggle was thus recorded on Kileen's walls for all to see.

The church's groups were strongly entrenched in Kileen and
there was even a level of cautious co-operation with Sinn Fein on
specific issues. Nevertheless the relationship was essentially one
of conflict and the church was confident of victory. 'Political
activity is practically dead on the estate,' the parish parish priest
remarked with some satisfaction.

4. Community Action

There are two community centres in Kileen, the Hollow Community Centre and the Acre Drive Community Centre, both responsible to Belfast Corporation. Their very existence promoted a range of community activities from bingo to youth clubs, especially in an area otherwise lacking in amenities. Hollow Community Centre claimed to be one of the busiest in Belfast; it was used by more than thirty groups, held daily advice centres, liaised closely with statutory and local agencies and was used as a base for repairs and complaints by the Housing Executive. Acre Drive Community Centre in southern Kileen was used by more than a dozen groups.

Not all these groups were well-supported or particularly active. The minutes of the Lower Kileen Residents' Association, which was formed in 1977, often referred to low attendances at meetings. In November 1978 a circular letter from its secretary announced a meeting to discuss winding it up: 'Interest in the Residents' Association has reached an all time low. The last committee meeting was attended by two committee members.' Part of the problem was the number of internal disputes and squabbles. The minutes of the Acre Drive Housing Action group, for example, described a meeting on 15 September 1976, when the chairman and some committee members resigned to form a local splinter association, which in turn folded. These splits and feuds were particularly conspicuous in 1976-8, just after new tenants, including squatters, had occupied the damaged houses vacated by Protestants. They were less evident in 1984, although there was no effective community group in the area.

Hollow Community Centre was generally regarded as respectable and conservative. Its close liaison with the church was shown by the fact that the church's groups often met in the centre; indeed one clergyman claimed that this support gave the centre its sole claim to have a real community base. The activists in Acre Drive Community Centre were much more radical and strongly anti-clerical. This dislike was reciprocated by the clergy. When the parish priest was asked to name the most serious threats to the stability of the estate, without hesitating to consider the conflicting claims of the Provisionals, the UDA or nuclear threat, he nominated the elements who operated from

Acre Drive Community Centre: they were 'disruptive', 'aggressive' and 'incompetent'; they did not provide leadership, but 'followed every whim and minority fad'. Another priest described the community centres as 'the worst thing that ever happened on this estate'. If the mutual dislike were disregarded, there was considerable agreement on both sides about the basis of their disagreements. For example, the appointment rather than election of officers to the church committees was attacked by the community activists as undemocratic, but was defended by the church as providing the leadership so absent in Acre Drive.

The difference in approach between the two community centres was partly a reflection of different views about the nature of professional community work. In Hollow Community Centre there was an emphasis on the importance of developing good working relationships with official agencies. The radical views held in Acre Drive led more often to confrontation, especially with housing and welfare bodies. For some, their republicanism made it difficult to co-operate with state agencies but their commitment to local needs required it. Some therefore preferred to retain their independence by remaining outside Sinn Fein, despite having to swallow accusations of 'selling out to the establishment'. One local social worker described the latter as 'the bare-footed social workers', and suggested that their aggression was often counter-productive. To the activists in Acre Drive, however, collaboration with the agencies too often amounted to selling out. The difference was epitomised by the outraged remark by one Acre Drive regular about Hollow Community Centre: 'They call in the police if there is any trouble at the centre.'

The Upper Ashbourne Estates

Relations between Catholics and Protestants

In 1984 the level of segregation and polarisation in the Upper Ashbourne estates was greater than in Kileen/Banduff. While this may have originally emerged from the violence of the early 1970s, subsequent paramilitary violence and mutual fear had prevented any blurring of the sharp boundary between Catholic and Protestant districts. The wasteland of derelict houses along the Vestry Road reduced the temptation to travel across it, and the tendency in both areas to look towards their own separate communities for work and pleasure made such temptations rare. The result has been the evolution of two closed systems. Apart from a small number of mixed-marriage families, no Catholics lived in Everton/Vestry and no Protestants lived in New Hull/Avoca. Nor was there any significant non-Christian minority to confuse the issue.

It is not surprising, therefore, that cross-religion friendships were hard to find. Nevertheless some relationships had survived the thirteen years since the time when New Hull was an integrated community. 'I still have friends from New Hull,' one woman said, 'but they hate it up there since we left.' One Everton resident claimed that he still visited old friends in New Hull, 'but not in the evenings'. Most admitted that meetings were only possible outside the Ashbourne area:

> There's no way I could go to their house in New Hull and they would be scared to come to my house [in Everton]. So we meet downtown, and still have plenty to chat about. It would be nice to see my old house again.

While there was sometimes considerable bitterness about the events which led to the Protestant evacuations in 1970, the blame was invariably laid either on 'outsiders' from Kellytown and other neighbouring Catholic estates, or on local Protestant 'agitators' who had persuaded people to move against their better judgment. 'They panicked the people' — exactly the same phrase used by one 'victim' of the UDA evacuation of Banduff estate — was the term used to describe the role of the local 'agitators' in New Hull. Some pointed to particular individuals, and this claim was made about a local loyalist political leader: 'If he hadn't come up, we would still be there.'

There were no shops or other amenities along the 'peaceline' in Upper Ashbourne, as there were in Kileen/Banduff, and there was no inclination or occasion for people to shop in 'hostile' territory. Both communities were served by different formal and informal transport systems. Most local workplaces also had sectarian connections, deterring people from seeking employment outside their own community, even if more jobs were available. In effect each community was self-contained for its transport, recreational and domestic needs.

On the face of things the presence of Stanley school — a Catholic primary school with a largely Protestant management committee and a mixed staff — suggests an ideal opportunity for cross-religious contact. In practice the Protestant members of the committee had few other occasions for developing relationships in Avoca or New Hull, and their collective and individual contacts were confined to formal school business. None of the teachers, Catholic or Protestant, lived in the estate, so the classroom offered no opportunity for community interaction. In other spheres where neighbouring communities might be expected to share activities — sports, cultural or cross-religious organisations, non-political interest groups like Gingerbread, the association for single-parent families etc. — the North Ashbourne estates either operated separately or not at all. One explanation for this remarkably low level of contact may be the absence of a community centre in the Catholic estates. Everton Community Centre had a variety of contacts with Catholic community centres in other parts of Belfast. Its boxers frequently visited Catholic clubs and they were visited in turn; a holiday was organised between Everton and a Catholic community centre in another part of the town under the Community Relations Holiday scheme. Contacts with Catholics had also developed through Citizens' Band radio and pupils from Catholic schools on the Falls Road had visited the centre. Whether the existence of a community centre in New Hull/Avoca would have encouraged similar co-operation is speculative. Cross-religious co-operation may only have been possible from a distance.

However great the lack of spontaneous co-operation between Protestants and Catholics in Upper Ashbourne, it might be expected that the public agencies servicing the area — the social services, community services, the education authorities, Belfast Corporation and the Housing Executive — would provide an overarching structure for people from both communities. In fact the structures of the major agencies were so arranged as to accommodate the religious division. The two communities were serviced from separate housing and social services offices, and Belfast Corporation Community Services Division used the terms 'Catholic west Belfast' and 'Protestant west Belfast' to distinguish its provision in the area. The separate public services, therefore, acknowledged the strength of the central division and did not provide even a formal opportunity for the two communities to meet.

Inside Protestant Everton/Vestry:
Internal Relationships

As far as the local clergy know, there are no Catholic families living in either Everton or Vestry, although there are about a dozen families of mixed religious background, few of them practising either religion. The Presbyterian church and the Church of Ireland are the two largest denominations.

The foundation stone of the oldest Protestant church in the area, the Church of Ireland's Luther church, was laid in 1838. The events of 1970 brought its activities to an abrupt end. Its rector between 1969 and 1974 described its new difficulties:

> The Luther church and hall were repeatedly damaged by vandals, and it became very dangerous for the parishioners left in the neighbourhood to either attend services and meetings because of the isolated situation of the little church in a by now almost completely republican area.
>
> (Cunningham 1978, 9)

The church was deconsecrated and its furnishings removed to St Anselm's church on the Jackstown Road. Men of the parish then demolished the church and hall.

St Anselm's, now the church for Cragban parish, is situated just outside Everton on the pleasant Jackstown Road. In 1984 it had 670 families, including both the privately owned houses north of that road, and Everton and Vestry estates. A number of organisations were based around the church — uniformed organisations like Scouts, Guides and the Boys' Brigade, old people's groups and two youth clubs. None of these was well attended from the two estates. Neither St Anselm's nor any other church was mentioned spontaneously when residents talked about activities in the area. When asked about the churches, most residents knew little about their amenities and few expressed interest in them. One local minister described the two estates as 'a mission field' where religion and churchgoing were peripheral activities. This view was supported by church attendance figures. About 200 parishioners out of a nominal 3,500 attend St Anselm's on Sunday, for example, 'and that is a highest point'.

What sort of activities, then, constituted the organised community life of Everton/Vestry? A Glasgow Rangers Supporters' Club was sufficiently popular to be able to restrict its membership to 150. Separate community associations had been formed at different times in Vestry and Everton and both had collapsed as a result of internal feuding. Vestry Community Association was formed in 1976, but was largely the creation of one family and supported by 'Peace People types'; the UDA tried to take it over, the original founders left and the association folded. In Everton a community association had been formed in the mid-1970s and played a part in the campaign to build Everton Community Centre. But shortly afterwards strong splits developed between individual members, Belfast Corporation took over the running of the Centre and the association dissolved. As in Vestry there was a paramilitary dimension to the feuds.

The Ulster Defence Association was the dominant, indeed the only, effective paramilitary body operating in the two estates. In 1970 the Upper Ashbourne had been one of the areas in which the UDA first became active. Road blocks were established then 'to protect the area against republican invasion'; some of the barricades remained, unmanned and obsolete, until the Department of the Environment removed them without protest a decade later. The UDA's interest in infiltrating Vestry and Everton's embryonic community associations demonstrated that its power, at least to disrupt, continued into the 1980s. By 1983, following a period of relative stability in the general area, there was an uneasy equilibrium within the UDA between the elements which favoured a strong organisation which could enforce its authority in the community and against outsiders, and those who wished to become more involved in conventional community action. The activities of the former group were marked by its public emphasis on retribution for petty crimes in the community: in 1983 a number of glue sniffers were punished; two separate robberies, in the Church of Ireland rectory and the Community Centre, were investigated by the UDA, the property returned, and 'disciplinary action' taken against the offenders. The weaker 'welfare interest' wanted to move the UDA towards involvement in such local issues as un-employment, housing and the problems of old people. Sometimes it attempted to co-operate with statutory and community services through the community centre, but on other occasions its attempts to dominate youth and community organisations created tension with the agencies.

The difficulty facing social and community workers, who were often willing to work with the 'welfare interest' in the UDA, was the high degree of overlap between its two functions. Thus the rooms in which they might meet to discuss the problems of the young people in the estates might also be used for storing guns or as 'romper rooms' for punishing offenders. There were also constant disputes about cash and suspicions about how it was being spent. 'You can only sup with the devil if you use a long spoon', according to one voluntary community worker who eventually found the exercise too indigestible and withdrew from co-operation with the UDA.

The internal struggles about the law-and-order role and the welfare role within the UDA were not peculiar to Everton and Vestry, but appear to have been endemic in both loyalist and republican paramilitary organisations. In the two estates, however, while extraneous factors such as UDA policy were important in determining the relative strengths of the two factions, the critical factor was the leadership at local level. More important, although the dispute was a real one within the UDA, it was quite possible for both types of activity to go on simultaneously.

The formation of Everton Community Centre in 1978 created a focal point in an estate which had lacked one. By 1983 it was widely used by a variety of organisations and interests, among them a playgroup, youth club, library, women's groups, discos, bingo, a CB radio club and a boxing club. A great deal of this energy had been latent before the centre was built. Disputes and shifting allegiances were a constant feature and many of the groups were shortlived.

Vestry had no community centre, although a small Community Services Centre was built in 1981. Its main function was to centralise local services, and the Housing Executive, social services and Citizens' Advice Bureau worked from the centre. A small informal group hoped to convert the centre from a services facility towards the more active encouragement of a greater community spirit in Vestry; the employment of an ACE worker was seen as a crucial first step towards this. When asked if there was much demand for such a development, a local community organiser replied that there was 'a strong need, but no demand'.

The provision of a Community Services Centre in Vestry, despite the proximity of a well equiped community centre in Everton, demonstrates the sense of separation betwen the two Protestant estates. Part of the case for building it, and the later case for developing it, was that children from Vestry 'were not made welcome' in the Everton centre and 'were looked down on'. The willingness to differentiate between the two estates was persistent on both sides. For some Ashbourne residents the bitterness dated back to the New Hull evacuations of 1970. Most refugees preferred to settle in Everton rather than Vestry, mainly because it was farther from the source of violence. As a result, according to one social worker, 'Vestry was implicitly regarded as buffer territory — even as expendable'. One Vestry resident felt that Everton had turned its back to them. 'They couldn't care less what happens to us.' By 1983, although parts of Everton had an occupancy rate as low as Vestry's eighty per cent, it was regarded as a superior area and the split dating back to 1970 was thus strengthened by perceived differences of social class.

This split only represented the primary division. Residents of both estates also made sharp social distinctions between the upper northern houses and the houses closest to the Ashbourne Road. In Everton this coincided to some extent with a distinction between those who had lived longest in the estate and the later arrivals. Loyalty to the estate as a unit was reactive rather than positive. If fights broke out at discos in Everton Community Centre between young people from Everton itself, the loyalties were localised and strong. However, although there were no Everton gangs as such, groups have been formed on an *ad hoc* basis to avenge attacks from Shankill, Glencairn or other areas outside the estate. 'They stick to their own', as one youth leader put it.

The internal fragmentation in Vestry was even greater than in Everton. It had originally, if briefly, been regarded as a high status estate and was popular with its first tenants. The violence which followed led to a speedy transfer of what one local clergyman described as the 'good people', and their replacement by squatters. Subsequent attempts to encourage community cohesion had been frustrated by internal dissention. Efforts to start a youth club excited little enthusiasm. In July 1982 even a collection to hold a party for children on the estate caused divisions among residents, with dark murmurings of earlier collections 'going astray'; eventually two parties were held, one for the upper and one for the lower parts of Vestry. Social contact between the two was low. An old lady from lower Vestry, whose son had been accidently shot dead ('My son spilt his blood here and that's why I'll stay') knew no one at all in Everton 'and very few from the upper part of Vestry'.

In these circumstances, any element holding together the precarious community was exceptionally important for the few activists in Vestry. The announcement in 1982 that Dunnock primary school in Vestry was one of the twelve schools scheduled for closure as a result of economic cuts led to the formation of the Dunnock Parents' Action Committee. For some of these parents the futures of the school and the estate itself were inextricably intermeshed. Certainly the former had provided a barometer of the latter's well-being. Built in 1970, it received its first pupils in 1971, including sixty-eight evacuees from Stanley school in New Hull. A problem facing the small school was the presence of four other Protestant primary schools within walking distance, all of them outside the estate. Parents had a wide choice for their children and exercised it. Children from the small Blackwater community to the south of Vestry, for example, attended no fewer than five different primary schools. Dunnock primary school fought a tenacious battle for survival, but its population had gradually dropped to a low of 186 in 1980 before steadying.

One community worker pointed out the implicit divergence between the school's educational viability and its importance to the Vestry community. Educationally there was no shortage of alternative schooling. The closure, however, was a major threat to an already disspirited community. 'It it goes, the children will go to a good school in the Jackstown Road, but this community will die.'

So the predominant impression of the communities in Everton and Vestry was one of social fragmentation. Both were seen by a local minister as quite distinct from his more prosperous parishioners who lived outside the estates. Within the estates Everton and Vestry were universally regarded as separate communities; in both estates, residents on the Ashbourne Road side felt that they were regarded as inferior by the people in the Jackstown Road side. Indeed the fragmentation went beyond these differences, for there was a strong local loyalty to even smaller areas — to a group of streets, to a street and, in at least one case, to part of a street. Despite efforts by community and social workers, people have resisted pressure to become part of a single community. There has been greater willingness to differentiate than to find common cause.

The internal divisions within Everton/Vestry were regarded as a serious obstacle to the area's recovery by most of its leaders and activists. These were explained in a variety of ways. One older resident in Everton pointed out that most families in both estates had moved from the Shankill area, with its variety of loyalties to the Upper Shankill, the Hammer and other localities; for him the current disharmony was largely the inheritance of the Shankill's territorial suspicions. Another view, expressed by a community worker, was that the antipathy to Catholics which had been aroused by the violence of 1970 had developed into a general insularity of attitudes and a suspicion of their co-religionists. Others blamed the planning and layout of the estates, with the absence of any central focus and the peculiar house-surrounded squares in Everton which encouraged incestuous neighbourhood loyalties. Nor was cohesion facilitated by the agencies and amenities in the area. Transport to the city centre operated from different edges of the estates rather than from inside them. Dunnock primary school's role as a unifying influence was diminished by the pull of other schools outside the area. Shops, pubs and recreational amenities attracted residents from the area, not into it.

So efforts to encourage a 'community spirit' were undercut by these powerful influences which eroded the unity sought by many activists in the area. In the end, however, it is difficult to escape the truism that the fragmentation resulted from the absence of any apparent feeling or need for greater cohesion by the people who lived there. The interesting question is whether this reflects apathy, or the view that the need for vigilance and solidarity against republican violence had diminished with the passage of time. The lack of community energy, especially in Vestry, favours the former analysis.

Inside Catholic New Hull/Avoca:
Internal Relationships

'Everybody in this area has to feel they have someone to look down on,' a man from New Hull stated. Certainly it was a community very conscious of internal distinctions. Ashbourne Park occupied the upper end of the social scale. Most of these privately owned houses had been vacated during the violence of the early 1970s and had remained unsellable for years. Eventually the Housing Executive bought and renovated them and, by a process of selling or letting, attracted people back to them. By 1984 Ashbourne Park was fully occupied, and the 'For Sale' and 'Sold' signs indicated some revitalisation of the area. Residents of Ashbourne Park, however, did not see themselves as members of New Hull/Avoca. According to a local teacher, parents there were 'more interested in their children', by which she meant more active in school affairs. According to some Avoca residents, people in Ashbourne Park had an air about themselves.

Although there was some social interaction between New Hull and Avoca, the two estates were distinct in many ways. When the Avoca Housing Action Committee (AHAC) was formed in 1981, for example, a group in New Hull attempted, unsuccessfully, to establish a separate committee rather than amalgamate with the AHAC. Part of the distinction arose from differences in the nature of the two populations. A considerable number of families had lived in parts of New Hull for more than a decade, giving it a more settled atmosphere. It was regarded as a step above Avoca by tenants in both estates.

Avoca's general social and environmental problems marked it out as the least popular part of the Upper Ashbourne in 1984. A particular block of flats, known locally as 'the welfare block', was the most dilapidated part of Avoca itself. Most of the occupants of the block were single-parent families, many of whom were unable to secure transfers of accommodation because they were in rent arrears. Living with them in the flats were two nuns who ran seven of the flats as a hostel provided by the social services, considerd by the Eastern Board to be one of their better-run hostels; between 1978 and 1983 more than 600 families had passed through the hostel. This represented the most deprived part of a generally deprived area.

The activities of the nuns reflected a significant change in the role of the Catholic church in New Hull/Avoca since the early 1970s. Quite apart from the Stanley incident, the parish of All Souls had a history of dispute between radical local clergy and a conservative hierarchy; one local priest had been in constant and public disagreement with two bishops for more than a decade, and there had been an attempt to transfer the nuns from the area. For these reasons, and as part of a general decline in religious observance in Catholic west Belfast, the church's influence declined greatly during the 1970s. By 1983 a local priest calculated that attendance at Sunday mass by the 580 New Hull/Avoca families who were nominally Catholics had fallen below thirty-three per cent. Non-attendance had lost its stigma. Indeed there was some social pressure, especially on men, not to attend. Those who did were described disparagingly as 'holy Joes'.

Since the late 1970s there had been a marked increase in church activity in the area. The nuns were its vanguard. They had moved into New Hull/Avoca in 1973, having been working in Kellytown but becoming aware of the appalling conditions in the other estate from the frequent calls for help from the St Vincent de Paul society, a church organisation concerned with social problems. They began to work with the local priest in St Anthony's multi-purpose hall, the only community focus in the area before 1984, which became a centre for dancing, mothers' and toddlers' groups, women's groups, bingo, courses, classes, a thrift shop and other activities. It was also a church, the altar separated for most of the week by a curtain. A temporary structure beside the hall provided the only setting in the estate for residents to meet informally for a chat; it was well used, especially by women.

So the church was launching a spirited attempt to win back its parishioners. Leading the attack were the nuns, who were universally popular. The strategy was one which involved the church much more than usual in the social life of the community. It was also one which involved a radical commitment to social change. By 1983 this new approach had done much to improve the church's image in the area, but not to the extent where people attended its religious functions as they had a decade earlier. It also involved the church more directly with political and community groups in the estates.

Provisional Sinn Fein had become the dominant political group in the area, although the Workers' Party and the Irish Republican Socialist Party were also active. Despite the personal popularity of its local representative, support for the Social Democratic and Labour Party (SDLP) was low. One illustration from a 1983 election meeting in Kellytown was quoted to explain this: the Sinn Fein and Workers' Party candidates appeared in their working (or casual) clothes, but the SDLP representatives, wearing suits and dresses, demonstrated by their appearance that they shared neither the class nor the community of the voters. Political allegiance stood for a lot in the estate and carried over to social relationships, but co-operation was possible on certain issues. For example, when the Avoca Housing Action Committee began its campaign, elected west Belfast representatives from Provisional Sinn Fein, the SDLP and Alliance worked together in support of their aims. This seems to support the view expressed by one of the local nuns that, despite bitter rivalry, the political groups could get together 'if the issue was important enough to the local community'.

There was also tension between the church and Sinn Fein and on one occasion, when workers on a cemetery gate were stoned by local youths, they were condemned from the pulpit. Sinn Fein was blamed for not controlling their own members. 'Sinn Fein build up hopes,' according to one local priest, 'but they are unable to deliver the goods.'

The security presence was high, with frequent patrols from Montgomery Hall, and little respect was shown by the army for local susceptibilities. A visiting priest conducting a mission in St Anthony's church was ostentatiously searched, and the army refused a request to halt traffic on the Ashbourne Road to allow a church procession to cross it on its way to Kellytown chapel. This latter event, when soldiers were alleged to have insulted the processors, caused considerable bitterness but no surprise. Despite this, paramilitary activity in the estate was low, but not unknown.

There was a subtle distinction between local attitudes to the army and to the police. Both operated from the heavily fortified Montgomery Hall, which was an army post and a police station. The army patrols were either ignored or hated. The police were regarded in a similar way when they were engaged in their para-military function, and it is almost impossible to imagine anyone informing them about a political crime. However local people used the police station quite regularly to report burglaries or other non-security crimes. 'There's no touts here,' one local resident claimed, 'but life goes on and you have to accept realities. Anyway, the insurance people need a police report.'

With the exception of the Avoca Housing Action Committee, the foundation of which was the result of exceptionally poor housing, the level of community activity was low. When the nuns set out to 'build up the community' through St Anthony's hall, 'there was a great lack of confidence' and it was difficult to start even the most modest community enterprise. There were few organisations, according to one activist, 'because they tend to become political, so people leave them'. Certainly whatever non-political activities were going on came to a halt during the hunger strikes, and Sinn Fein had on occasion tried to take control of any community initiatives. There was an attempt to take over the Avoca Housing Action Committee, for example, but Sinn Fein was eventually persuaded that they should keep out. 'Campaign with the groups, but do not create them' was the prevailing Sinn Fein policy in 1983, but more than one community activist in the area was apprehensive that it may change. Indeed a more active involvement in 'community politics' by Sinn Fein, with its para-military connections, would certainly create problems for community workers employed by official agencies. In practice any popular movement in New Hull would be likely to reflect the Sinn Fein sympathies in the estate, so the advantages of a more overt role for Sinn Fein may be outweighed by the problems it would create.

Despite the unpromising environment and the low level of morale, there was general agreement that conditions had improved since 1980. As evidence of this people pointed to the demolition of the Avoca flats, the building of the St Anthony church and hall, the opening of the large leisure centre in nearby Cragban and the youth club. The nuns believed that the incidence of family violence, especially wife battering, had declined significantly. It would be a considerable exaggeration to claim, however, that New Hull/Avoca enjoyed a reasonable quality of life.

Stanley School 1970-83:
A Case Study

Northern Ireland's primary and secondary schools are highly segregated by religion, more than ninety-eight per cent of Protestant children attending Controlled primary schools and an even higher percentage of Catholics attending Maintained schools (Darby *et al* 1977). Consequently, when Stanley primary school was built in 1963 to serve the population of New Hull, its Controlled status reflected the predominantly Protestant population of the estate. The main Protestant churches controlled more than half the places on the school committee and all the teachers were Protestants. In 1983 the principal, who taught in the school since it opened, estimated that about twenty per cent of the school's population in 1969 were Catholics, but the actual figure was closer to eight per cent. The other Catholic children in the estate attended St Aidan's and St Bridget's schools on the other side of the Ashbourne Road.

The rapidity of the Protestant evacuation from New Hull in 1970 created peculiar problems for Stanley school. Its population, which had risen steadily to 630 children in September 1969, had shrunk to 218 when the school reopened on 1 September 1970, and most of these came from outside New Hull. Thirteen teachers lost their jobs. Further decline seemed inevitable.

Among the new arrivals, however, were the children from six Catholic families who had moved into the houses vacated during the summer. Their motives for sending their children to a 'Protestant' school were varied. Some were concerned about their children crossing the busy Ashbourne Road to attend the nearest Catholic schools. Some claimed that they had been told that these schools were already overcrowded and could accept no further pupils, and the 933 pupils attending St Aidan's at that time give support to this view. The convenience and good reputation of Stanley school was a more positive factor. It is difficult to assess the claim that some parents were motivated by concerns relating to community relations, but such claims were made at the time (McEldowney 1970) and repeated in 1984. Whatever the reasons, the response of the Catholic church was speedy. At an emergency meeting called by the clergy in St Bridget's school on 20 September parents were told that their children could not receive adequate preparation for the sacraments of Communion and Confirmation at a Controlled school, and that they should be withdrawn. Most obeyed.

In November the parents of those children who were still in Stanley asked the local curate to give religious instruction to their children. When this was refused they themselves paid an unqualified teacher to provide instruction. The school authorities, who had stood well back from the controversy, permitted this, and preparation for Communion and Confirmation began. As the bishop of Down and Connor was to officiate at the latter ceremoney on 24 March, the issue was bound to become public. The bishop, perhaps hoping that the problem would resolve itself, refused to meet the parents and attempted to purchase the school from the local education authority. However, after pressure from the local curate, from the Community Relations Commission which had assisted towards the cost of paying the teacher, and from growing media interest, he eventually agreed to the secondment of a teacher of religion from a neighbouring school three weeks before the Confirmation ceremony. It was the first occasion upon which a Catholic teacher of religion had been appointed to a Controlled school in Northern Ireland.

The departure of the Protestant population from New Hull during this period obviously affected the school population, and by 1972 Stanley had become the only Controlled school in Northern Ireland with an exclusively, or even a predominantly, Catholic population. The anomaly was that the school management committee still represented the same interests as it had in 1963 — the Church of Ireland, Presbyterian and Methodist churches and the local education authority. Only the three parental representatives who sat on the committee in 1983 reflected the altered religious distribution of the school's population. On the other hand there had been an undramatic evolution from an entirely Protestant teaching force in 1970 to one of sixteen Catholics and three Protestants — one of them the principal — in 1984.

In 1984 the school reflected the poverty of its environment. Of the 338 pupils attending in 1983-84, 250 received free school meals on the basis of family poverty. The security presence was as obsessive as the poverty. Patrols were frequent and the army post/police station in nearby Montgomery Hall was a focus for violence during every period of political turmoil. Even in normal times vandalism was endemic. After the 1983 summer holidays every window in the school had been broken and the erection of steel shutters was insufficient to prevent repetitions. Break-ins were regular, lead was stripped from the roof, plumbing pulled from the walls and floors flooded. Despite all this, the predominant atmosphere in the school was one of order and liveliness. Parents in the estate spoke warmly of the school and its teachers, although questions were being asked about why so few pupils progressed to grammar schools, and attendance at Parent-Teachers' meetings rarely exceeded twenty. Nevertheless the high regard for the school was partly a reflection of the school's success in accommodating to the contradiction between its Controlled status and its Catholic population.

For a Protestant school the main organisational problems in accommodating to Catholic pupils arose from the central position claimed for religious preparation and practice in the Catholic view of education. In Catholic schools, holidays were arranged to allow for feast days, preparation for the sacraments was an important component of religious education and unscheduled visits by clergy were frequent. None of these were customary in Controlled schools. Nevertheless the management committee of Stanley had already begun to adjust to the new reality by 1970, when it permitted the teacher employed by the parents to use the school. By 1971 an unusual compromise had been reached over the church's requirement that children attend mass on holy days of obligation when Controlled schools usually stayed open: school met as usual, but the roll was not called until lunch time, thus allowing the Catholic children to meet both religious and educational demands.

By 1984 the process of accommodation had advanced considerably. On holy days of obligation Stanley closed. The peripheral disruption which accompanied preparation for Communion and Confirmation was accepted, and Catholic clergy often visited the school, the local priest saying, 'I'm in and out all the time'. Yet the principal and management committee were still Protestant. The changes had been reached with considerable skill and understanding from all parties involved and all expressed satisfaction at the outcome.

Stanley school attracted considerable attention in the media in 1970, when the sight of Catholic parents defying church leaders suggested to some observers that a wind of change was about to engulf Irish Catholicism. A thoughtful article in the *Irish Times*, for example suggested that the conflict

> revealed a degree of militancy on the part of those Catholic parents involved, about 100, and a preparedness to stand up to the church authorities, which has not been evident among Northern Catholics in recent years. . . . This is undoubtedly one of the side effects of the Civil Rights agitation. . . . By agreeing to Miss McKenna's teaching of religion as a subject on the school curriculum, however, it [the church] may have created a precedent which will be difficult to ignore when the debate on integrated education increases.
>
> (McEldowney 1970)

In fact the Stanley case did not open the floodgates and release a strong popular demand for integration. No other school has followed the model since it was established. The real significance of the episode is to be found in the period following 1970, with the unpublicised but successful search for an accommodation between administrative structures and popular pressure. It is all the more remarkable for developing in a community where other cross-religious contact was virtually absent.

Dunville

Relations between Catholic and Protestants
It is a cliché that many people in Northern Ireland claim

acquaintences among the opposite religious group. 'Some of my best friends are Protestants.' Nonetheless the frequency with which it was claimed in Dunville contrasted with the two communities studied in Belfast. Protestants were particularly anxious to claim that they had 'stacks of Catholic friends', and were also more likely to look back to pre-Troubles times when, they often claimed, schools were more integrated and people helped each other out at potato harvest and in times of need. More Protestants also advocated educational integration, a local policeman suggesting that 'if you have gone to school with your neighbour, you're not going to kick the lining out of him'. Catholics more often remembered grievances and niggles from these earlier times, but all were concerned that Dunville should be regarded as a friendly town, now and in the past.

It is difficult to gain a general impression of the extent of cross-religion freindships in the town. Donnan and McFarlane have pointed out how in Northern Ireland 'baptisms, weddings and funerals . . . are principally the concern of kin', but how 'when it comes to less direct involvement in rituals, this clear boundary between those who should be involved seems to become a little blurred' (Donnan and McFarlane 1983, 120). Wakes and funerals were generally attended by all affiliations in Dunville and it was not unusual for people to attend weddings and christenings outside their own churches. Perhaps the high proportion of mixed marriages in the town necessarily involved a greater degree of participation in family events than was common elsewhere.

In 1984 the pattern of organised activities in Dunville reflected a community conscious of its religious divisions in some activities and able to overlook them in others. Churches, schools and political groupings were highly segregated, while voluntary and sporting groups often had members from all religious groups. This is an artificial division; the churches, for example, were heavily engaged in sporting and voluntary activities. Nevertheless there was a tendency in formal organisations towards segregation, while those activities which engaged people from both sides were more likely to be informal.

There were no fewer than forty-six churches for less than 30,000 people in the Dunville council district in 1983, six of them in the town. They were its most important source of organised activity. The largest congregation was Catholic, followed in turn by the Presbyterians, the Church of Ireland and the Methodists. A number of small Protestant evangelical congregations had overlapping memberships with the main churches and, according to some clergymen, took every opportunity like bereavements or illness to 'poach' their members; they were rarely mentioned by other ministers when religious activity in the town was discussed.

All the churches were extremely active in sponsoring social and sporting activities. Sunday schools, choirs, scouts, guides, Boy's Brigade, Women's Associations and Mothers' Unions all operated from church halls. By far the most popular activities run by the churches, however, were bowls and youth clubs; one bowls club claimed 540 members. Within the Protestant community there was no strict parochialism in supporting these clubs. It was quite common for members to belong to clubs of different denominations because they preferred the atmosphere or because the meetings were at more convenient times. There were even Catholic members of clubs attached to Protestant churches, but little traffic in the opposite direction. Clergymen from the main Protestant churches often attended functions in each other's halls, but not across the sectarian divide. The town's bowls clubs played in two leagues — the Churches' League which was exclusive to the Protestant churches, and the Mid-Ulster League, which was non-denominational.

Co-operation between the Protestant ministers was not confined to attending bowls competitions, although some of them stressed that this sort of informal contact was important. The local primary school attended by Protestant children had been formed by an amalgamation in 1967 of a Church of Ireland and a Presbyterian school, and its management committee represented both churches. Exchanging pulpits was common between Protestant ministers. Some of the ministers had been told by parishioners of regular meetings between the town's clergy to defuse possible trouble in the town 'before my time', but none knew why they had stopped. Certainly families who had been intimidated in 1983 were almost unanimous that the town's clergy had made no significant intervention to affect what was happening, and one at least was embarrassed by their failure. 'I'm afraid our influence is very small.'

Despite the opinion of one teacher that the local Protestant clergy 'ranged from cultured men through to party fanatics', clergy from all the main churches expressed sympathy with the idea of co-operation between Catholic and Protestant congregations, with only minor qualifications. One Protestant clergyman said that 'for me, to be a Protestant does not mean waving a Union Jack on the Twelfth'. Another claimed that he would find it easier to have a Catholic priest in his pulpit than a minister from one of the small proselytising Protestant sects. This latter remark was more an expression of his contempt for the 'missions' than of any serious intention ever to invite a Roman Catholic priest to his church. 'If I did that,' he pointed out, 'I would alienate half the parish.' He went on to add: 'You have to lead, but you have to bring people with you — the aim is to stay one step ahead.' Another minister was more caustic about the prospect of closer co-operation with the Catholic parochial house: 'It's difficult enough to get the Presbyterians together.' The views of the Catholic clergy were equally tolerant, and equally wary. As a result, contact between Catholic and Protestant clergy was largely confined to the politeness of casual meetings and occasional chats at funerals. Caution lay under the expressions of good will.

Dunville has two primary and two secondary Maintained schools for Catholic children. Protestants attend one primary and one secondary Controlled school. Segregation is almost complete, although the technical college and the WEA classes were well integrated. There were only thirteen Catholics among almost 800 children attending the Controlled primary school in 1984, and an even smaller proportion of Protestants in the Maintained schools. There was a convention between the secondary schools whereby pupils wishing to take 'A' level subjects which were not available in their own school could take them in one of the others. This had emerged from the expressed wishes of parents and had created no problems, but only a very small number of pupils took advantage of it.

Co-operation between the schools was minimal. No regular sporting contact took place between them, although there had been joint sports days in the past, stopped for no reason anyone could remember. The Police Community Relations branch tried to encourage co-operation through intermittent road safety quizzes and sporting competitions, but there was hostility among some Catholic parents about the police coming to the school. There had been protesting telephone calls from parents following a 'Top of the Form' competition and a school had been ransacked after one of them. Nevertheless the police claimed that a Superstars competition held in Protestant and Catholic schools after the formal school day had ended had been very successful, and that a woman constable was welcome in all the schools to give regular talks on community relations. Other community relations projects, including rambles, weekend camps and a project involving fifteen children from Ranafast and fifteen from Limedrop, were also supported: 'I could have taken one hundred if we had had the money', according to the local Community Relations policeman, who believed that their success was based on personal contact and the fact that the projects took place outside school hours. Such initiatives were possible in Dunville, according to the same policeman, 'but I wouldn't even attempt them in the hardline country areas like Ardboe or Pomeroy'.

The limits of co-operation were delicate even in Dunville. A concert organised by Protestant and Catholic Encounter (PACE) during the high tension of 1980 was a dramatic failure, with the Protestant schools pulling out. 'We have the parents to think about,' stated one teacher. 'Fear of disapproval from parents and clergy' was often mentioned as a major deterrent to co-operation between the schools, suggesting that the tolerant views expressed by the clergy during interviews were sometimes not carried into practice. 'You can't make teachers the scape-goats for the divisions in this community,' said one teacher, 'and you shouldn't look to them to mend them.' The failure of the PACE concert was explained by one principal as the result of cooling relationships during the build-up before the H-blocks campaign, but he was unable to quote evidence of prior warmth or subsequent reheating.

The schools are physically close and there was some satis-faction that, although the children got out at the same time, there had been no violence of the sort associated with some neighbouring schools in Belfast. Shortly after this was quoted to me as an example of tolerance in the town, an incident took place which illustrated how precarious it was. A bus-load of children from the Catholic school was passing through a neighbouring village when the funeral of a murdered UDR man was taking place, and obscenities and political slogans were directed towards the mourners. An extraordinary meeting of the school management committee was called and an unequivocal apology offered, along with an explanation that the bus had been deliberately scheduled to avoid the funeral but the plans had gone awry. People in Dunville were well aware of how easily such incidents can lead to more serious conflicts.

One political party in the town is unashamed in its opposition to closer co-operation between Catholic and Protestant school-children — or adults for that matter. Pressure from the DUP was widely blamed for the PACE debacle. In an interview with a researcher, a local leader confirmed that

> he would be totally against any efforts at forcing school-children of differing religions to mix or co-operate with each other. He also said that if he were aware that such efforts were continuing in the town he would make strong representations, as he had done in the past. He was sure that he would have the backing of the majority of parents in the town for this.   (Mullan 1984)

This uncompromising stand caught the tone of political interaction in Dunville. Election campaigns for the local council were less concerned about amenities or local issues than updating the local head count — particularly vital in Dunville, given its population balance. The tone of council debates has changed very little over the last two decades but has been sharpened since 1969 by the spread of violence. It was a frequent complaint that, when intimidation seemed to be threatening the very nature of the community in 1981, none of the local councillors attempted to defuse the situation, many preferring to exchange accusations and insults. The central unionist-nationalist rift has lost its comforting simplicity in recent years with the rise of the Democratic Unionist Party and Provisional Sinn Fein. The divisions within the two religious communities have come to rival the divisions between them. Even during the height of the hunger strikes campaign, when pressure for unity was greatest, the DUP and the Official Unionist Party were competing for unionist support; there were rival unionist counter-protests against H-block demonstrators in April 1981. In 1984 the OUP held a narrow majority of four to three over the DUP — the eighth unionist belonged to a smaller party — but enough to give it the chairmanship. Preparations for the 1985 campaigns had already begun in 1983.

Matters are scarcely less complicated on the nationalist side. In 1984 the Social Democratic Labour Party (SDLP) held the majority of the opposition seats. 'This has never been a republican town', according to a local priest, indicating that Catholics had found the conservative nationalism of the SDLP more to their taste. A measure of this view has been the willing-ness of nationalists to contact the police both for routine complaints and for protection, a phenomenon almost totally absent in some surrounding republican areas. There was unease among some Catholics in the town that the events surrounding the hunger strikes, and the new arrivals into the town since the 1970s, may have disturbed this pattern. The newcomers are often characterised by older residents as 'out-and-out republicans', and there is genuine uncertainty about the level of support Provisional Sinn Fein might have gained. One local politician claimed that the Sinn Fein Advice Centre attracted little support and believed that even Clanmor would vote SDLP, but others felt that nationalist support might be fairly evenly divided between the two parties. The 1985 elections confirmed their judgment.

At ground level overt paramilitary activity has been low in the town itself since 1981, although violence has continued in the surrounding countryside. In December 1983 the security situation in the town was judged by the police to be sufficiently stable to remove the barriers which had blocked the main street to traffic for more than a decade. Despite this the number of attacks on property in the town has not increased. Occasional incidents, which may or may not have a sectarian undertone, still continued, but only became a serious threat to order in the weeks before the annual Twelfth of July processions. The bands and procession which paraded during 'the marching season' still caused nervousness on both sides of the divide.

The tradition of 'banding' in Northern Ireland, especially in connection with the Orange Order, has long been accompanied by violence. A distinction was often drawn between 'respectable' bands and 'kick-the-pope' bands. The former were often church-based and distinguished by their orderly marching and restraint in playing party tunes; the latter were 'loyalist rather than Protestant' as one Protestant opponent put it, had younger members and were marked by their aggressive repertoire and behaviour. Three Protestant Dunville clergymen independently mentioned the 'Boyne Heroes' band from Ranafast as a source of serious provocation in the town, although one mentioned that the Catholic Gaelic Athletic Association (GAA) bands could also be offensive to Protestants. The Dunville band was a 'kick-the-pope' band, distinguished by its willingness to provoke by marching into Catholic streets. Cromcastle Park was a favoured venue in Dunville, and one unauthorised invasion led to police firing rubber bullets to exclude them. The purpose, in the words of a minister, is 'to rub their noses in it'.

It would be misleading to consider the denominational, educational and political disunity as characteristic of Dunville. Activities in the town were broad enough to balance the segregated organisations with activities and clubs supported by both Catholics and Protestants. The number of sporting clubs in particular is remarkable: in 1983 there were five soccer clubs with a total of six teams in the Mid-Ulster League; at least six bowling clubs, only some of them church-based; camogie and Gaelic clubs; clubs for cricket, athletics, boxing, hockey, motor-cycling, squash, swimming, table tennis, pool, snooker and angling; an eighteen-hole golf club. The religious breakdown of the people who supported these clubs may shade in one direction or the other; camogie, Gaelic football and boxing, for example, were Catholic games in Dunville; cricket and one of the soccer teams had a largely Protestant following. Given the central sectarian split, however, religious affiliation seemed to play little part in Dunville's sporting life and the recreation officer described sport as 'a positive factor for co-operation'. In the view of a local youth worker, the presence of so many activities in the town further contributed to stability by providing activities for unemployed young people and helping to keep them off the streets.

The commercial and professional middle classes have also been responsible for a familiar spread of clubs and associations.

There were active Rotary, Round Table and Lions' clubs, and the golf club was often mentioned as a social venue in which Catholics and Protestants could meet socially. Two of the school principals, one Protestant and one Catholic, were members of the golf club committee, and this was thought to encourage a tolerant atmosphere. Working class social clubs were harder to find. There were no tenants' associations in the town, nor much taste for the sort of activities carried out by community groups. Membership of the British Legion and the Irish National Foresters cut across social barriers, but could not be said to do the same for religious divisions.

The tendency for voluntary associations in parts of Northern Ireland to drift towards denominationalism has been observed by Rosemary Harris (1972) and Susan Starling (1970). They described how support from one religious group sometimes deterred members of the other from joining. In Dunville the restraints were less severe and a number of voluntary and interest clubs claimed memberships across the religious board. One example was the Gingerbread group for single-parent families in Dunville. This group was formed around 1976 at the initiative of a social worker, and for two years had only five members. By 1984 there were about thirty members, mainly from Dunville but including people from thirty miles away. An average attendance was about twenty-five. Their main function was to support each other and their children and they were actively associated with other similar groups throughout the province. Rather more than half the members were Catholics.

It is curious that one particular segment of single-parent families — those produced by murder or imprisonment arising from the Troubles — had not joined the Gingerbread group in any numbers. Among the members 'sectarian issues are never discussed; they never come up', according to one founder member. 'We have too many problems in common, like bringing up the kids.' When asked to consider the problems of running a mixed-religion group in Dunville, the only incident remembered was some slight tension between Catholic and Protestant youths at a disco they organised during the hunger strikes. One member went on:

Some of our side and some of theirs were intimidated. I've

never heard them discuss it. In fact, this is the first time I've talked about it myself.

Protestants and Catholics in Dunville had joined Gingerbread because they shared common problems. There were also institutions in the town specifically designed to improve community relations. The police Community Relations branch and the PACE group have already been mentioned; both were highly specific, and the PACE group was only periodically active. Political parties — like the Alliance and Workers' parties — which emphasised the importance of community relations and courted all religious groups attracted little support. Neither contested the local elections in May 1981 and, in the Fermanagh-South Tyrone by-election of 1983 their combined support came to just over four per cent of the poll. In general, therefore, those organisations which set out to bring together the town's factions have been conspicuously less effective than those which started from a point of common interest, and whose cross-religious support was incidental.

The Effect of Violence on Relationships

The violence of 1981 has left some people with very bitter feelings. 'This is a small town,' one man pointed out, 'and everyone knows everyone, including those who were the intimidators.' Suspicion did not die quickly. While seeking an address in Ranafast, I was approached by three residents while still in my car, asked politely about my business and watched carefully until I was accepted into a house. The most bitter feelings came from Protestants. One woman, while favourable to the principle of co-operation with Catholics, admitted that it was 'hard to forgive them for what they are doing to our people in the security forces'. Many were unable to understand how their Catholic neighbours could condemn violence, but not inform the police about the plans of the paramilitaries. That such plans are fairly widely known by Catholics was a common view among Protestants — denied by every Catholic interviewed — so Catholic reticence was often put down to hypocrisy, fear or a general spinelessness.

Families with members in the security forces — and few Protestants did not have some relation or close friend involved — were particularly nervous and suspicious. One woman with a husband in the RUC reserve said, 'I just cut myself off and don't think about the danger; but it's not natural, is it?' Another described the way in which membership of the Ulster Defence Regiment had affected her husband's life and that of her family:

> He doesn't talk much about it, but any knock on the door at night still frightens me. Every day he has to try to take a different way to work and he always carries a gun. We hardly ever go out in the evening — it's just too much trouble thinking about where we could go that was safe. It's probably not worth all the trouble — if they set their minds on getting him, there's not much can be done to stop them. . . . Yes, we have Roman Catholic neighbours and we get on well together. Still, you can't help wondering what they are thinking, the way things are at the moment.

The need for constant vigilance was a major theme for such families. One Protestant policeman, who believed that there was no point in trying to build bridges between Catholics and Protestants until the security situation had improved, talked of the extravagant over-drinking and behaviour when he and his colleagues left the district for a holiday or course. 'You just can never relax around here.'

The different attitudes among Catholics and Protestants towards the violence did reflect a fundamentally different view of community membership. Even for Catholics who disapproved of IRA violence, uniformed and armed policemen and UDR men were clearly regarded as actively engaged in a war. They may not have been 'legitimate targets', in the IRA jargon, but there was less sympathy for them than for the civilian victims of sectarian attacks on members of the Catholic community. For Protestants the murdered policemen and UDR men were both metaphorically and literally members of their community. Both groups were, at least in part, reacting to the violence as members of different communities.

People have adopted different methods to deal with the traumatic events of 1981. Avoidance is one of these. 'We don't often talk about it,' one woman said, and a policeman who had been brought up in the town explained:

There's no fighting, no open antagonism, but very few strong friendships [between Catholics and Protestants]. Under drink, they will sometimes talk about what happened in 1981.

Others took care to make distinctions between the minority of local people who were actually engaged in the intimidation and the majority who disapproved of it. The clearest expression of this view came from a Protestant woman who said, pointing out the difference between Catholics who supported the IRA campaign and the 1981 intimidation and those who opposed them: 'We call them "the bad Catholics" and "the good Catholics".' It is not unusual too for Catholics to distinguish between the DUP supporters and other Protestants, the sectarianism of the former often dismissed with an amused shrug of the shoulders, or as pure gut bigotry, requiring no further explanation. The possibility of blaming it on outsiders, as happened in Belfast, was not available in such a close community. But one variant on this search for scapegoats was to look for culprits among the newcomers who came into Dunville during the 1970s. One older Catholic resident said, 'It's no coincidence that the trouble started in Clanmor. Sure they're not Dunville people at all.'

The result of all this has been the emergence of a kind of consensus in the community that things might have been a lot worse. 'It was shivered and shook and looked like breaking,' in the dramatic words of a Catholic curate, 'but it didn't.' There is a cautious, and perhaps vainglorious, optimism about the future, and pride in the resilience of the past. One man who had actually left his house because of threats boasted of Dunville's moderation: 'If this was Dungannon they would have shot it out rather than move.'

8.

Contact after Intimidation

THE EXPERIENCE of every community which suffered intimidation was unique, yet all went through similar cycles involving a build-up, a climax and a period of adjustment. The climax was that period in the crisis when antagonism between Catholics and Protestants reached a peak of intensity — when relationships were almost entirely negative. By 1984 fourteen years had passed since this climax in the Upper Ashbourne, eleven since the worst tension in Kileen/Banduff, and three since the worst events in Dunville. Such levels of violence and distrust cannot be sustained indefinitely, and by 1984 all three had arrived at some form of accommodation, or at least a lower level of tension. The physical closeness of Catholics and Protestants in all three communities both intensified mutual fears and made some form of contact between them almost unavoidable.

What forms of relationship or contact evolve between conflicting communities after intimidation has run its course?

Simmel believed that every conflict which did not progress to genocide implied some form of social activity between the combatants (Lawrence 1976, 139). Any attempt to assess this by a simple measuring of demographic integration misses out the variety of contacts which take place even in the most segregated community. On the basis of the three districts studied, however, it is possible to classify the post-intimidation contacts between Catholics and Protestants in four main forms: contacts through personal relationships; contacts through organisations; contact resulting from sharing common institutions; and contact resulting from sharing neighbourhood amenities.

1. Personal relationships

Most community studies stress the exceptional importance of

kinship in determining personal friendships in Northern Ireland; Donnan and McFarlane regard it as a major cause of segregation:

> Segregation derives much more from the fact that people emphasise the importance of kinship and to a lesser extent neighbourhood relations for ordering everyday contact and co-operation.   (Donnan and McFarlane 1983, 134)

Although Kileen/Banduff and the Upper Ashbourne estates were built in the post-war years, each estate was populated to a large degree from cohesive communities in the older part of the city. This colonisation preserved the kinship and friendship networks and, despite the more abrupt changes created by intimidation during the 1970s, social relationships remained essentially local in 1984. Social visiting between Catholics and Protestants within both Belfast areas was almost non-existent. The only friendships which crossed the sectarian frontier were those which dated back to pre-intimidation days in New Hull; and all meetings between these old friends took place outside the area.

Nor did mixed marriages between Catholics and Protestants provide a social bridge in Belfast. In his survey Richard Rose found that only four per cent of his 1,291 sample had married across the Orange/Green divide (Rose 1971, 341), and Harris, in her study of Ballybeg, concluded that 'intermarriage bridged no gaps'. When violence broke out, mixed marriage families were among the first to leave such polarised communities for more integrated areas, and were among the early targets of intimidators. Those who remained identified closely — sometimes extravagantly — with whichever of the two communities among which they had elected to live. The tensions raised by intimidation forced everyone to opt for one side or the other. An ambiguous position was untenable.

Cross-religion personal friendships were more common in Dunville, and the number of mixed-marriage families was also greater. While the violence of 1981 reflected the growth of tension between Protestants and Catholics during the hunger strikes, it also generated alarm about the effects of a sectarian split in the town, and anxiety to prevent its repetition. What distinguished this from similar, but unsuccessful, concern in Belfast in the early 1970s was the broader base of cross-religious contacts before the intimidation itself. Many of these contacts survived the violence, and some of them may even have been strengthened by the vision of disruption presented during 1981. Nevertheless, an increased wariness between Catholics and Protestants still existed three years later, along with uneasiness about how well the town would stand another similar bout of violence.

2. Organisations

The level of contact between organisations in Dunville was much greater than in the two Belfast communities. Although polarisation in the town had been deepened by intimidation, there were still opportunities for contact between Catholics and Protestants. They often belonged to the same clubs and societies and worked in the same offices and factories. So it was at least possible to form relationships either within one's religious community or with people from the other group.

Such opportunities were less common in the two Belfast districts. All voluntary groups were formed from one side of the divide and there was virtually no contact across it. Similarly with recreation and community centres: although the community centre in Protestant Everton had developed links with other Catholic centres in the city — to the point where groups of children holidayed together — there was no relationship with the Catholic community on their doorstep. Even though there were Protestant members on the management committee of Stanley school which was mainly attended by Catholic children, this had not led to any cross-religious contact in Upper Ashbourne. Clergy in the areas rarely met each other.

The main exceptions to this lack of organised cross-religious contact were economic ones. All three districts had exceptionally high unemployment, and the poor job prospects for young people was one of the outstanding local concerns. This concern was sufficient to make the Shamrock workshop in Kileen attractive to Protestant youngsters from Banduff, despite its location in what they openly regarded as hostile territory. The management committee, the instructors and the young people attending the workshop represented both communities and there were few signs of tension. In Dunville too it was in the interest of shopkeepers, businessmen and the local press to maintain the town's attractiveness as a commercial centre and to smooth over the animosities created by intimidation.

3. Common institutions

While schools and churches in Northern Ireland serve a segregated community, people in all three districts were all serviced by the same housing authorities, social services agencies and local councils. The existence of a bureaucratic infrastructure for all citizens, Catholic and Protestant, might appear to provide a setting for contact between the groups.

They did to some extent in Dunville, but all the major agencies provided separately for 'Catholic west Belfast' and 'Protestant west Belfast'. In both Banduff/Kileen and the North Ashbourne estates, the Housing Executive, Belfast Corporation and social welfare agencies all had separate offices for both communities. These were staffed by different workers. So even the low-level contact offered by visiting the same office or dealing with the same social worker was not available. In the provision of public services, a policy of apartheid operated in west Belfast.

4. Common amenities

The importance of amenities and facilities — shops, pubs, transport offices — in creating a common view of community is sometimes underrated. A key explanation of the negligible contact between Catholics and Protestants in North Ashbourne was the absence of any amenities which were used by both groups. For these facilities, Catholics and Protestants travelled in opposite directions.

In Dunville, with the exception of facilities provided by churches and political organisations, amenities were common property. Even in Kileen/Banduff, which experienced such a protracted and bitter confrontation, the presence of shops along the sectarian frontier not only contributed to reducing tensions, but also led to a mild erosion of suspicion; by 1983 some people in both communities were attending social and commercial activities arranged by churches from the other side. The presence of an infrastructure of such amenities does not ensure that association takes place, but its absence removes even the occasion for contact.

All four points of contact were actual or potential forms of social activity, but were not equally important. There was a progression in their quality. At its extremes, this progression ranged from personal relationships to incidental contacts, from chosen meetings to incidental ones, and from altruistic relationships to those arising from common problems. The importance of contact, or lack of it, was demonstrated clearly in the range of attitudes expressed by people who lived in communities which had been affected by intimidation: every contact, forced or chosen, created some sense of allegiance to a common community; lack of contact between communities, especially those which were geographically close, encouraged both ignorance and fear. Personal friendships and co-operation between groups were more likely to encourage greater stability within an area which had experienced high levels of intimidation and sectarian violence. The peculiar mixture of contacts along the scale had led the three areas to quite different forms of accommodation.

In 1984 Dunville remained essentially a cohesive community despite an increase in residential segregation and a popular view that relationships had become more polarised. Three years after the town's experience of intimidation, contact was still taking place at all four levels, although the centre of gravity may have shifted down the scale. The question is: why?

In the first place, unlike Banduff and the Upper Ashbourne, there had been a long history of religious integration in the town and a tradition of regarding it as a unit. Shops and offices were patronised by all religious groups. Pubs, clubs, and recreational facilities were, with minor reservations, treated as community facilities. Even the local newspaper, while essentially unionist, made efforts to report Gaelic football matches and was read by Catholics. While not commonplace, neither was there a taboo on cross-religious attendance at christenings, marriages, deaths and wakes. All of this provided a common infrastructure within which the two main denominational sub-structures could relate to each other while also maintaining their separateness.

When sectarian disputes did come to a head, they were often contested in a highly ritualised manner. The council chamber was the most obvious arena for these formalised exchanges. During council meetings routine matters were despatched with reasonable efficiency. However there were other issues — the granting of late licenses or debates on security or housing plans — which triggered off quite predictable and unproductive exchanges of insults and accusations. None of the exchanges was intended to convert councillors from the other side — basic allegiances were uncomplicated by the possibility of floating voters. Nevertheless, despite their relative impotence, the minority members — always outvoted, deprived of committee memberships and generally frustrated — still continued to attend and to affirm their membership of the community. It is difficult to avoid the conclusion that these rhetorical clashes had two functions only: to demonstrate to one's supporters that the flags are being proudly flown, and to let off steam within a controlled setting. Better an encounter at the lists between the champions of the two groups than a civil war.

The behaviour surrounding the holding of potentially violent processions and parades was also highly conventional. There was a convention that people have a right to hold them; there was a convention that they should be strictly limited to particular streets and estates — as clearly defined by graffiti as the markings of an animal's home ground — where the co-religionists of the marchers predominated; there was a convention that 'a few hot-heads' each year attempted to extend the limits of their stamping grounds; there was a convention that such encroachments must be resisted by their opponents; and there was a convention that the police be stoned by one side or the other or both. Hence the rules which regulated the town's differences were dusted off annually and tested. When an incident went beyond the limits, as when the Catholic pupils abused the Protestant mourners in 1984, the breach was clear to most responsible people in the town and the instant apology succeeded in calming matters down and confirming the boundaries on decent behaviour.

These intermeshed and ritualised conventions, relationships and structures were distinctive to Dunville and evolved as the town itself evolved. There were undoubtedly similar processes in most other towns in the province to deal with regional variations in the Catholic-Protestant relationship. In Dunville the central

point was that they implied some level of willingness to preserve relationships in the town in spite of a rupture like that
of 1981.

The high level of polarisation established between the North
Ashbourne estates during the early 1970s, on the other hand,
had scarcely been affected at all by the passage of time. In 1984
the Protestant and Catholic estates were still almost completely
segregated at every level. The most striking contrast between
this area and the other two was the absence of common acceptable mutual amenities in which Catholics and Protestants could
shop and have the opportunity for even perfunctory contact. It
is unfair to criticise planners for not having considered this
when the estates were constructed, and perhaps optimistic to
imagine that such amenities would have survived the violence
in the area during the early 1970s. But the absence of a non-
political common ground has made a cautious realignment of
the type that happened in Kileen/Banduff impossible. Instead
the separation between the two groups has become institution-
alised. The high level of violence along the 'peace line' of the
Vestry Road in the early 1970s led to the divorce. The absence of
any facilities which both sides could use, and the endorsement of
the division in the procedures of the official agencies, made it
final. The attitude of the divorcees towards each other was not so
much hostility and fear as the lack of interest which springs from
long separation.

A major obstacle to a reunion was the obvious truth that
the divorce had produced, in purely local terms, a high level
of stability. The ten years since 1975 had seen less sectarian
violence than the previous five. For people who lived through
the trauma of 1970, this was a gain to be valued. The price of
the stability, however, was greater insularity and introversion
within the communities, and the possibility of larger-scale
sectarian confrontations in the future. It seemed to many people
a price worth paying for immediate security.

Relations between Protestant Banduff and Catholic Kileen
were much more dynamic than in the other two communities.
The period of defensive polarisation in Kileen/Banduff,
following the intense population movements before 1976, had
allowed both communities to adjust to their changed circumstances. It also led to important changes about how people

within their sectarian laagers came to regard their own communities and that of the other group.

The high levels of consensus within both Kileen and Banduff has already been noted. In Kileen a considerable base of political, religious and cultural sympathy — most strikingly demonstrated by the revival of interest in Irish language and culture — contributed to a strong common identity. This was less marked in Banduff; nevertheless people there shared a strong support for loyalist political parties as well as a common apprehension about its future as a Protestant estate, which encouraged a sort of defensive unity. The consensus which had grown, separately, in Kileen and Banduff provided comfort and confidence. It also encouraged an introverted local chauvinism which for some residents was rather claustrophobic. One unemployed Banduff Protestant talked of his 'feeling of being hemmed in a box', a description frequently repeated in other terms by other residents. A youth worker in Kileen expressed it more dramatically: 'Some of these kids, if they stepped off the Falls Road, would think they were abroad.'

As the definition of their communities became narrower in both Kileen and Banduff, it inevitably became more distinctive and sectarian. The very definition of community values — Protestant and loyalist in Banduff; Catholic, republican and Gaelic in Kileen — excluded, either consciously or implicitly, the other side. Thus physical polarisation was followed by ideological polarisation, and there was ample evidence in both communities of both ignorance and dislike of their rivals. The reactions of one young Catholic community worker whose family had been intimidated and who had moved into one of the vacated houses in Acre Drive may serve as an example: after the completion of the interview, she asked if this research would also deal with Protestant victims of intimidation. When this was confirmed she asked, with genuine interest, where such people were to be found. When it was pointed out that some of the Protestants who had previously lived in Acre Drive believed that they had been forced to leave their homes, her reaction was a mixture of disbelief and anger. It did not match her definition of intimidation. Some of her neighbours were more sympathetic, or at least ambivalent, towards the Protestant victims of the Troubles, but their sympathy for the Protestants who had been forced to leave Acre Drive was tempered by their own experiences of overcrowding in Kileen, and by the needs of Catholic victims of intimidation from other parts of Belfast. They were also the victims, so tolerance was limited.

Consequently, while many people prefaced their remarks by distinguishing carefully between paramilitaries and 'ordinary people' on the other side, the distinction was often forgotten in the conversation which followed. The common belief among Protestants that Catholics knew when attacks on the security forces were about to come clearly implied active collusion between the gunmen and the general Catholic population. So one result of local polarisation was a growth in mutual distrust, as rumours had become more difficult to check.

Despite the high level of physical and social segregation in Kileen/Banduff, people had begun to use some common amenities and, in limited situations, to work together. Clear distinctions were made between the situations in which co-operation was possible and those in which it was unacceptable, and the discrimination was determined primarily by the function of the activities: voluntary or altruistic contact — personal friendships, voluntary organisations — was rare: but contact which offered a concrete advantage — the community workshop, convenience of shopping — happened more frequently. Even when it prospered, however, as with the co-operation between the schools, there was an awareness of the dynamic and delicate nature of the relationships and of the limits to what could be attempted. Relationships had changed since the antagonisms of the early 1970s, were still changing in 1984, and held the possibility of further changes in the future.

It is optimistic to imagine that time always softens the edges of polarisation. Fourteen years had left New Hull as polarised as it was after the evacuations, yet some of Dunville's wounds had begun to heal after three years. In some respects Kileen/Banduff was the most interesting case. Although segregation was still high, some relationships had developed through a combination of common amenities and the fact that tenancies became more stable. The leaven of time meant that people had more to lose from a recurrence of violence.

9.

The Strengthening of the Heartlands

IT WOULD be a mistake to exaggerate the level of rapprochement in any post-intimidation community. If polarisation is defined as 'a situation in which all positive bonds are within blocs and all negative bonds are between them' (Jenkins and Smoker 1971), all three districts became more polarised in the period following intimidation. Visits between Catholics and Protestants became more difficult; friendships more rare; the level of interdependence diminished. In Belfast the focus of people's concerns became more narrow, concentrating on the local estate rather than the broader district. Community groups showed less interest in such abstract ideals as peace or co-operation than in practical and sectional needs. Community activity and community disputes were more likely to be internal rather than external.

The urban tendency towards sectional living was not peculiar to Belfast, Timms even claiming that 'the physical isolation of differing populations seems an inevitable concomitant of urbanism as a way of life' (Timms 1971, 2). This may be too sanguine a view when applied to Belfast's experience. Kuper was less optimistic, describing polarisation as a process by which the harmonious relationships which occur even in plural societies are driven out, and internal divisions are accentuated. Social structures and ideologies become more exclusive and more simple, aims are perceived as irreconcilable, and violence often follows (Kuper 1977, 240). In west Belfast the segregation which accompanied this process was created by both external and internal forces. The external pressures were powerful, direct threat or violence often forcing isolated minorities to seek refuge in the heartlands. Having been forced to move, however, there were strong internal pressures to remain, arising not so much from intimidation against political nonconformists as from an awareness of the social consequences of leaving — ostracism from one's own community and suspicion from the other.

There were more positive reasons too. There is plenty of evidence that urban ghettos, cemented by the institutions and rituals which were exclusive to them, provided fellowship and comfort before 1969. For Harbinson, the Orange Order, with its status hierarchy and its annual celebration on the Twelfth of July — 'How wise of William to win his battle at the height of summer, so that festivities in its honour through the centuries after could be held in sunshine and fine weather' (Harbinson 1960, 125) — provided a major childhood bond. The rituals and the 'secret password' which he swore to keep from all other ears upon joining the junior Orange Lodge marked the membership of a club which often ended only with the member's death. Devlin and McCann, although both scathingly critical of the Catholic Church, acknowledged that it wielded a similar power, and attributed it to the church's dominance in Catholic social and political life: McCann depicted the local *Derry Journal* newspaper as a miniature *Osservatore Romano*, whose editorials fulminated against birth control, the Communist threat and general immorality of the day. The link between the Irish Catholic Church and republicanism was absolute. 'We came very early to our politics,' wrote McCann; 'one learned, quite literally at one's mother's knee, that Christ died for the human race and Patrick Pearse for the Irish section of it' (McCann 1974, 9). The sectarian school system was regarded as central to this process of acculturation. Not only the nationalist traditions passed on within Catholic schools but, as McCann put it:

> There were men in the area who embodied the tradition — Paddy Shields, Neil Gillespie, Sean Keenan, Old Republicans who had fought in the past and been jailed and whose suffering represented a continued contribution from our community to the age-old struggle.
>
> (McCann 1974, 10)

According to Harbinson, Protestant schools also fostered an exclusive pride in the group's values, although he himself rejected it:

Crowding out any other aspects of history, our schools drummed into us over and over again the Protestant story. On leaving school, and none too early for my liking, I had no notion of the world's past other than a few prehistoric tales and dreary details concerning our Protestant faith and the unrelieved darkness of Rome. The particular rack on which they tortured us appeared in the form of a small, buff-covered booklet entitled 'How we differ from Rome'.

(Harbinson 1960, 121-2)

This sectarian socialisation was helped greatly by the two sides' mutual ignorance of their opponents' beliefs and practices. Harbinson, for example, went on to describe the speculation among his schoolmates about how much money Catholics were required to pay to have their sins forgiven, and the fear and hatred of the pope in Sandy Row. He continued:

In spite of such entrenched opinions, our ignorance of the Catholic world was profound. I, for instance, believed that Mickeys existed only in parts of Belfast and nowhere else except the Free State and Rome itself. That many Catholics were living in London, or were allowed to live in London with our Protestant king, seemed impossible.

(Harbinson 1960, 131-2)

It is significant that most of these descriptions came from writers who grew up in the segregated heartlands. Most people in Northern Ireland, however, lived in more or less integrated communities. There is some evidence that such contact with alternative views modified cross-religious attitudes (see, for example, Harbison and Harbison 1980). Certainly Dunville's recovery from intimidation was more speedy than that of the two Belfast communities.

The subject of this chapter, however, is the growth of the Catholic and Protestant heartlands of west Belfast. Both Kileen/Banduff and the North Ashbourne estates were at the interface between them, and the boundaries were sharpened and confirmed by the events of the 1970s. The character and growing self-reliance of the heartlands owed much to their experience of violence and intimidation.

The move towards local self-containment, especially in urban areas, will be examined by exploring in more detail five of its main characteristics: natural community bonds; cultural and ideological exclusivity; internal divisions; maintenance of law and order; and relations with the agencies of the state.

Natural community bonds

Harold Isaacs believed that basic group identity was largely prescribed at birth:

> An individual belongs to his basic group in the deepest and most literal sense that here he is not alone, which is what all but a very few human beings fear to be. . . . It is an identity he might want to abandon, but it is the identity that no-one can take away from him.
>
> (Isaacs 1976, 35)

In a society with strong sectarian conflicts, and occasional violence, territory plays a major part in defining group identity. Leyton, Harris and others have pointed to a common regional loyalty in rural districts, and to what the former called 'shared values' between Catholics and Protestants. Certainly both Catholics and Protestants in Dunville still regarded themselves as belonging to the same town; the town's relatively speedy recovery from the effects of intimidation was partly due to a common desire to preserve an integrated community.

However group identities in Belfast were much more localised, according to Harold Jackson, even before the violence of the 1970s:

> The church is plainly the focal point, and then the school. Around these two buildings cluster the population they serve, and so a ghetto is born.
>
> (Jackson 1971, 10)

Certainly the parish was often the main unit but it was just as likely to be one of the city's traditional communities or a new housing estate. Indeed, as in Banduff and Kileen, the new estates were largely populated from cohesive communities in the old city. So the religious and ideological patterns were passed on despite the onslaught of modernisation, as the heartlands expanded by colonising the suburbs.

One effect of violence and intimidation in the city was a

strengthening of these local loyalties. Minority families moved or were removed, and the boundaries between Protestant and Catholic communities were sharpened and clarified by the removal of the mixed streets between them. The result was that it became much easier to define and recognise one's enemies: they were the ones who had left, the ones who lived on the other side of the boundary, the ones whose fellows had intimidated and killed your fellows. Their visible distinction made it more difficult to fudge the issue of where one's primary loyalty lay.

Cultural and ideological exclusivity

The different means by which both Protestants and Catholics defined their culture — sports, literature and music among them — have often been remarked (see, for example, Harris 1972 and Leyton 1975). Since the outbreak of violence in 1969, and particularly since 1980, there have been clear signs of what Beals has described as cultural revitalisation movements — 'deliberate, organised, conscious efforts by members of a society to construct a more satisfying culture.... They are the reactions of people to stress and disillusionment resulting from contact with a dominant culture' (Beals 1967, 237-238).

So it is not surprising that this growth of conscious pride in membership of a distinctive cultural group has been particularly marked in Catholic areas. It has taken many forms. There has been a greater tendency for people to refer spontaneously to an interest in Irish history, sports and culture. This has led to a revival of interest in the Irish language. Graffiti written in Irish began to increase from 1980; in some estates, like Twinbrook from 1981, hand-painted street names in Irish were added to the official English language signs; a group of young Irish speakers started printing an Irish language paper called *Preas an Phobail* (*The People's Press*) in 1980-81 to encourage its use. By 1983 there were at least twenty-five Irish language classes, mainly for beginners, in Catholic west Belfast, perhaps double the number operating in 1979. Some of these were held in Gaelic Athletic Association (GAA) clubs which also encouraged social nights for Irish speakers.

This flowering of Irish culture had not sprung entirely from fallow ground: as early as 1971 the *Bunscoil*, an Irish language school, had been started by a small Irish commune in Shaw's

Road, close to Kileen. This was exceptional, however, and the low level of interest in the Irish language is indicated by the decline in the number of pupils throughout Northern Ireland taking it as a subject for public examination — from 2,460 in 1972 to 2,034 in 1978. Many of the people who began to attend Irish classes in greater numbers during the 1980s were not ex-Irish speakers who had dropped the habit, but people who were learning it as one would learn a foreign language. In the sense that the natural use of the Irish language had long disappeared in most parts of Northern Ireland, its revival was an artificial acculturation for the students. Their interest arose from a growing association between Irish culture and republicanism, especially since the hunger strikes which were often mentioned by language enthusiasts as the catalyst for the revival. Certainly it can be dated from 1980-81, and some of the teachers had themselves first learned the language while in prison during the 1970s. Sinn Fein encouraged its supporters to do the same. The association between language and politics was overt in *Preas an Phobail*, which adopted a strong radical nationalist position, and the importance of the language to 'the national struggle' was a constant theme in republican newspapers. It was expressed most succinctly in an advertisement in *Republican News* for Irish classes in 1973: 'The British Army speak English: What do you speak?'

It is not easy to find an equivalent cultural form in Protestant communities. The strength of feeling on some political, constitutional and religious issues is indisputable, but Protestant culture is most often expressed as a reaction against Catholic values and aspirations. Leyton, writing about the small Protestant rural community of Perrin, observed that its inhabitants 'see their village as a bastion of Protestant morality and Protestant virtue, stoutly maintaining their faith in the face of their Catholic neighbours who are associated not only with the freedom-denying monolith of Roman Catholicism, but also with Irish secret armies, with black magic, Communism and atheism' (Leyton 1975, 11-12). This stressed the relationship between religion and culture on the Protestant side. In the three areas studied in this research, all of which, unlike Perrin, had experienced exceptionally high levels of community violence, Protestants emphasised their political rather than their religious identity. Indeed religious activity was low, and doctrinal attacks on Catholicism were very rare. There was one major distinction between the cultural life of the Protestant and Catholic heartlands in Belfast, less noticeable in Dunville: for Catholics, culture was a set of views which were expressed in public activities like Gaelic sports, dancing, song and language; for Protestants there were no activities — apart from annual processions — to give substance and support to the set of views. This distinction may arise from the nature of minority communities which emphasise their cultural distinctiveness as compensation for what they regard as their exclusion from economic and political power. It may be observed, in different forms, among the Quebecois in Canada and in the 'black pride' movement in American cities in the 1960s.

This distinctiveness, which is less conspicuous outside the heartlands, became sharper as Catholic Belfast became larger and more insulated from the rest of the city. With this came a growing confidence of its own strength and independence, and an unwillingness to accept the values of other communities. It continued to share with Protestant districts the vehicles of a common culture — television, radio and newspapers, leisure activities — but placed greater emphasis on a culture which rejected British values and incidently excluded Protestants. It was a way of saying: 'We are strong enough to go our own way. If there is to be a settlement between Protestants and Catholics, it will not take place through assimilation, but by negotiations between two different cultures which inhabit the same space'.

Internal divisions

The shift of focus in Kileen from an external difference with Protestant Banduff towards internal divisions also has its roots in the growing confidence of Catholic west Belfast. No one seriously believed that the demographic changes which had made Kileen a Catholic community could be reversed. The high level of organised community activity and the open diversity of interests were indications of a strong confidence in its future. The low level of community activity in neighbouring Banduff indicated a continuing apprehension and the need to guard against internal dissention in the face of external threat. Even in upper Ashbourne, where community activity was generally at a low level, there were more organised activities in Catholic

Avoca than in Protestant Vestry. Catholic confidence which arose from membership of a strong Catholic heartland contrasted with the feeling among Protestants that they were at the border of shrinking Protestant territory.

The catalyst which had led to the most bitter divisions within Kileen was the emergence of Sinn Fein and its new interest in community politics in the 1980s. The establishment of advice centres and their involvement in housing and welfare rights issues created a visible and active presence, but was dismissed as a political ploy by an SDLP rival:

> They are only in it for cheap gains. They blame the Brits if they don't get what they want, and take the credit if they do.

Some other community activists and professional community workers were also concerned that Sinn Fein's real aim was to infiltrate community groups and that this would seriously retard community action in the city. In fact the level of Sinn Fein's involvement varied greatly between different communities. In some, existing community groups were hijacked by the manipulation of elections, and one such takeover in Kileen led to the collapse of the group; in others they were persuaded that they must co-operate with other interests rather than replace them.

The entry of Sinn Fein into communtiy politics may have been the immediate reason for the growing internal divisions, but the more fundamental causes were changes in the social structure of Catholic west Belfast during the 1970s. Before the Troubles, conventional leadership of the Catholic community was determined by the need for internal structural unity, aided by a general perception of hostile external forces — unionist control, gerrymandering and discrimination. Priests were important as community leaders, but were generally content to leave political leadership to trustworthy, conservative surrogates — the business and professional middle class and the Nationalist party. Direct clerical involvement in politics had been rare.

The decline of the SDLP in Belfast and the rise of Sinn Fein, especially since the latter began to contest elections in the 1980s, were serious challenges to this order. The surrogates were no longer delivering the goods. Further, for the first time, the decline in church attendance put into question the devotion of

Catholics to their church, previously taken for granted. This collapse of traditional political and religious structures in the Catholic heartlands was a matter of grave concern for some of the parish clergy. It has persuaded them that they must take a more direct leadership role. Priests have become more directly involved in job creation projects; indeed their willingness to use the state-financed BAN (Belfast Area of Need) and ACE (Action for Community Enterprise) schemes have made a significant contribution to youth employment. Nor was the renascence of parish-based groups, such as the 'environmental groups' which have been formed in parishes in west Belfast, spontaneous. It was part of a struggle for power within the Catholic communities, and the main antagonists were often the Catholic church — conservative, paternalistic, non-violent — and Sinn Fein — radical, anti-clerical and supporters of the IRA. The clergy in Kileen regarded radicals and republicans as greater threats to the stability of the area than any external enemies. The antipathy was mutual. In the republican press the main objects of attack, apart from the British army and government, were not unionists but those elements within the Catholic community which opposed republicanism. In an attack on liberalism in one republican paper, for example, the Peace People and Bishop Daly were accused of trying 'to destroy the Irish nation and Irish nationalism'; their view, it was claimed, was that 'the Provisional IRA must be crushed', because the Provisional IRA is the 'principal spiritual force' of Irish nationalism and the 'only armed force' which it has at its disposal (*An Phoblacht* 15 Lunasa 1975). The struggle came to occupy the attention of activists and there was a corresponding decline in interest in what was going on inside Protestant communities.

Traditionally the level of organised activities has been lower in Protestant communities. Neither the Ulster Unionist party nor the Democratic Unionist party had shown a sustained interest in community action, so it has not become an arena for political rivalry. Paramilitaries have occasionally shown some interest. In Everton, for example, the UDA provided virtually the only focus for community action. However its involvement has deterred others from becoming involved and has produced faction fighting and dissention. This rarely became public. The opposition was expressed in conversation, not in action. Overall community activity was lower than in the corresponding Catholic communities, and internal differences were not reflected in the creation of rival community structures.

It is possible to exaggerate the influence of paramilitaries on community groups. In most communities the number of activists was small, and both paramilitaries and community groups drew their support from the same constituency — the young and the unemployed. In many cases the overlap of membership simply made it unnecessary for the paramilitaries to organise election coups.

Maintenance of law and order

When Frank Burton carried out his research in Anro during the mid-1970s, many people in the community regarded it as a war zone. The IRA was expected 'to protect the community when Protestant gunmen fired directly into Anro' (Burton 1978, 83), and the community felt very dependent on their protection. Consequently, unless IRA actions in Anro attracted retaliation from the army, the paramilitaries could claim a mandate for their bombing campaign.

Ten years later the war was no longer the major pre-occupation of Catholics in the west Belfast Catholic heartlands. The concentration had shifted to a new internal emphasis on the need for effective law and order. Power and status in the localities were judged to a great extent on who was able to protect and police them. In the minds of most people this involved two separate if overlapping problems, 'the war' and 'ordinary crime'. In both Protestant and Catholic communities 'the war' was regarded as the struggle between the IRA and the security forces rather than a war between the communities. Consequently Protestants often stressed the need for more police and army presence to protect them and to wipe out the IRA, while Catholics were more likely to regard the British army as the interlopers and the cause of violence. A more fundamental difference was the willingness of Catholics to accept that those in uniform — the army, UDR and police — were more 'legitimate targets' than the Catholic civilians who were the victims of sectarian assassinations; many Protestants, especially in Dunville, had family members in the UDR and RUC, and regarded their killings as equally sectarian acts. Consequently Protestants were more concerned about the conduct of 'the war', as they perceived it as a greater threat to their community.

Catholic perceptions, especially in Belfast, were different: although some were committed to the cause — one quoted approvingly Pearse's view that 'bloodshed is a cleansing and a satisfying thing and the nation which regards it as the final horror has lost its manhood' — most people were less interested in ideology than pragmatism. They might disapprove of republican violence, but they had sympathy of its reasons. As Seamus Heaney put it, writing of punishment shootings, they

> ... would connive
> in civilised outrage
> yet understand the exact
> and tribal, intimate revenge.

> (Heaney, *Punishment*, 1975)

Far from dominating their lives, the violence rarely impinged on them. Often the immediate effect of increased polarisation was a reduction in levels of sectarian violence — more people have been killed in their homes in mixed communities than in segregated areas (*Belfast Telegraph*, 5 January 1980). The Troubles increasingly became something which went on outside the heartlands, actively conducted by a few, accepted as part of normality by some, opposed by others, but only condemned openly when it directly affected the life of the immediate community, which it rarely did. Otherwise most poeple preferred not to think about it. The heartlands provided an insulated refuge from 'the war', like the calm in the eye of the hurricane, an area of tranquility surrounded by violence. In such circumstances 'the war' was an abstract concern in comparison to more 'ordinary crimes'. The problems of joyriding, vandalism and drugs, especially for the young, were regarded as more serious than violence arising from civil strife.

For most Protestants the army and RUC carried the main responsibility both for winning the war and for dealing with normal crime; the role of the paramilitaries was subsidiary and exceptional. In the Catholic heartlands people made a clear distinction between the two types of crime. Few were prepared to have any truck with police or army in matters concerning 'the war'; but conventions were more complex when it came to ordinary crimes. Burglaries and attacks were reported to the police fairly regularly. But when it came to the crimes which most worried them — particularly those associated with young people like joyriding, drug pushing and the selling of alcohol to minors — people looked to whichever group seemed most able to prevent them. This included the police, the paramilitaries and direct community action. One of the most emotive problems in the Catholic heartlands during 1983 and 1984 was 'the hoods' — the young bloods who stole cars and drove them around the estates at high speeds at night. Despite sanctions from every quarter — prison sentences from the police, knee-cappings from the Provisional IRA, shootings from soldiers after driving through road blocks and a number of deaths through crashes — the hoods remained beyond control, and stubbornly prepared and able to continue their activities.

It was important for paramilitaries to demonstrate both that they could protect their communities against outsiders and that they were the effective providers of law and order within them.

The essential prerequisite for protecting their communities was the ability to maintain internal control and unity, and increased polarisation certainly provided an ideal setting for intimidating internal non-conformists into line. One anti-Unionist paper, while emphasising the need to destroy the Northern state, went on:

> But up until such a stage is reached it is vital that the anti-Unionists prepare self-defence. The Catholics of the East [Belfast] must not end up like the Jews of pre-war Germany who were led to the slaughter like lambs. Self-defence is an immediate priority.   (*Unfree Citizen*, 30 October 1972)

Paramilitary newspapers on both sides kept a vigilant watch for back-sliders. The loyalist press constantly advised its readers not to spend money in Catholic shops or pubs — often helpfully identifying them by name — or to buy anything produced in 'the potato republic'. But the worst sanctions on both sides were directed against informing to the police. Typical was the 'Warning to stool pigeons' which appeared in a loyalist paper:

A number of persons have been using the 'robot phone' in order to tip-off the security forces to loyalist arms caches. We warn these people that this is treason and will, if detected, be punished by the usual sentence for this crime.

(*Ulster Constitution*, 13 January 1973)

Feelings ran even higher against informers on the republican side. The tout, defined as 'an informer — a class of person remarkable for their short life expectancy' by the cartoonist Cormac (*Resistance Comix*, 5), was a major threat to the security of paramilitary organisations. In 1973 the republican newspaper *An Phoblacht* ran a heavily-stressed series of articles called 'The Informers', featuring Quisling and other historical villains. During 1983 and 1984 the names of supergrasses were abused on gable walls. The level of concern was reflected in the periodic amnesties offered by the Provisional IRA to informers, promising that 'any person who surrenders to the republican movement will be unharmed, provided that he or she is prepared to make a clean breast of what has occurred' (*Irish Republican Information Service*, 31 July 1974). Punishment was severe if they were caught: when the IRA reported their killing of two 'intelligence agents' in 1974, they were at pains to point out their objectives in questioning them:

Both men divulged a large amount of information, including the names and addresses of paid informers operating in Derry. Last night both men were executed.

(*Irish Republican Information Service*, 5 November 1974)

Law enforcement by the paramilitaries was not confined to crimes connected with the war. The UDA in Everton had adopted a policing role, recovering stolen goods and punishing the alleged thieves, and warnings against criminal activities often appeared in the neighbouring *Woodvale Defence Association News* (see 'The threat to housebreakers', *WDA News*, 30 November 1974). Once again, however, the most active intervention by paramilitaries came from the republican side, especially since the mid-1970s. In 1976, for example, the Provisionals promised to smash a 'children's crime ring' of eight to fourteen year olds by 'putting pressure on their parents' (*Andersonstown News*, 25 December 1976).

The most serious challenge to the paramilitaries' ability to control the level of ordinary crime came from the hoods. Public reaction against their joyriding and general lawlessness was high, so high that in 1984 a group of tenants in Kileen called on the IRA to execute them. While this may represent a momentary loss of balance, it is true that many people in the communities were embarrassed rather than appalled by the idea of knee-capping, preferring to turn a blind eye to it. However, when knee-cappings and systematic beatings were carried out against the hoods in the estate, there was strong criticism from many quarters. The most bizarre of these was the complaint that the use of hurley sticks in the beatings be-smirched the culture of Gaelic Ireland, which led to their replacement by baseball bats. These may have been more acceptable culturally, but the body of the complaints were directed to the more general concern of paramilitary groups overstepping their role. There had been concern about these law enforcement activities for many years (see *The Irish People*, March 1975). The main message appears to be that, while most people were hostile to the RUC, they were not prepared to have the IRA replace them without considerable caveats. At the same time, by intervening more frequently as a surrogate community police force, the Provisionals created expectations that they were able to police the area effectively. Hence their inability to deal with the hoods diminished their prestige.

One major difficulty was that paramilitaries did not seem able to make a real distinction between their treatment of 'security' crimes and what they called 'anti-social behaviour'. Similar sanctions — group beatings, knee-cap shootings, broken limbs — were applied to both, and at least two men were murdered in west Belfast for 'anti-social behaviour'. 'To compete with the ideology of the law,' as Burton pointed out about the IRA, 'it must establish that it is challenging the legitimacy of the law and not just breaking the law' (Burton 1978, 128). Bringing the violence into the community had a sharp effect on the popularity of the IRA and the INLA, and Gerry Adams of Sinn Fein attributed its defeat in the European elections of 1984 to losing 'those nationalist voters who may have had some misgivings about IRA operations in which civilians were killed or injured' (*Belfast Telegraph*, 7 July 1984).

Writing of the relationship between the Basque separatist movement ETA and the Basque community, the nationalist leader Xavier Arzallus compared it to a glass of beer: 'You find strength and fermentation in a beer, and you will get some froth on top. You can blow away the froth, but there is fermentation in the beer, and froth will reappear as soon as you move the glass' (Buschshluter 1984). The analogy applies to the relationship between the paramilitaries and people in the heartlands, but it is also true that, despite the general tendency to ferment, the beer may go flat if the conditions are not right. Fermentation cannot always be taken for granted.

The people who lived in the Catholic heartlands were not disinterested spectators in the struggle between the state and the paramilitaries to deliver law and order. The Provisionals started with the home advantage, but the support was conditional. If they could not produce results, or if their methods were unacceptably violent, they were strongly criticised. There were even occasions when the police, if not admired, might be used. The limits on the powers of paramilitaries can only be defined when they are breached, and there have been occasions when they have had to retreat or reconsider their tactics. Nevertheless, progression towards greater paramilitary involvement was greatly facilitated by the fact that the alternative forms of policing were not acceptable.

External relations

Within ghettos it is characteristic for people to seek control over as many of their own activities as possible. There is a realisation, however, that this aspiration towards complete independence cannot be achieved. As already described, each of the three districts studied reached its own level of inter-group contact, or avoidance. Relationships with the agencies of state were more difficult. There is some evidence that Catholics have greater difficulty than Protestants in identifying with political and administrative bodies in Northern Ireland (Burton 1981). Murray, writing about schools, described the close identification between Protestant schools and 'the policy-making and administrative sections of the educational system'; Catholic schools, on the other hand, regarded them more suspiciously, only contacting them 'on occasions of dire necessity' (Murray

1983, 148). Suspicion of state agencies was also evident in Belfast's Catholic heartlands, but contact was often unavoidable. In areas where unemployment was high and where most people lived in public housing, for example, it was essential to have a good working relationship with social welfare, housing and other public agencies.

For most individuals and community organisations this caused few problems. The success of the all-party Avoca Housing Action Group in securing the demolition of local maisonettes was based on a skilful campaign aimed at government ministers and decision makers in the administration. One of Kileen's two community centres had very close relations with all local agencies — indeed the housing authorities worked from the community centre. On the other hand some republicans had ideological objections to working with the agencies of the state. Further it was official policy for local authorities and the main departments of government to withhold recognition from Sinn Fein. This apparent impasse was in practice easily resolved. Regardless of what policy operated at the level of government, contact with Belfast Corporation, the Housing Executive and government departments took place for local people within their own areas in local offices. These were almost as much part of the local community as of the state bureaucracy, and indeed straddled the two. They provided the link between the heartlands and the administration. Thus, Sinn Fein's increasing advocacy role and its welfare rights surveys, while officially ignored, brought them into daily contact with the people who staffed the local welfare, housing and government offices. Relationships were often strained, sometimes hostile, occasionally close, but they constructed an *ad hoc* bridge between Sinn Fein's ideological abstentionism and the government's refusal to deal with people who advocated violence. They allowed the life of the community to function.

The retreat to the heartlands was an attempt to create a tolerable existence in what many people regarded as a violent and dangerous world. It had accompanied most periods of urban sectarian violence since the early nineteenth century. Indeed the periodic purgative of intimidation, while not the sole cause of segregation, was an essential agent in maintaining the

Catholic and Protestant heartlands. Seen as a defensive rather than an aggressive process, it had many positive qualities. It provided communities with a high level of homogeneity, it reduced the influences of outsiders — including 'the other sort' and the state — over one's life, and it encouraged a community and cultural life in which one could feel comfortable. 'Tall walls make good neighbours': behind them it was possible to construct a kind of normality amid the surrounding chaos and danger.

There was, of course, a price to pay. The same processes which encouraged internal strength and clarified group identity also relegated opponents beyond the Pale. The walls divided ideological as well as territorial communities. In its mildest form this encouraged a narrow parochialism, illustrated by the Kileen youth worker who observed that 'some of these kids, if they stepped off the Falls Road, would think they were abroad'. In Upper Ashbourne too parents were unwilling to let their teenage children out at night in case they wandered into the wrong area. At another, more serious, level increased segregation from the other side led to a narrow ethnocentrism, and an increased willingness to stereotype opponents. Both developed cultural and political activities and beliefs which excluded the other. Lack of sympathy soon followed lack of knowledge, as with the young girl who refused to accept that any Protestants had been forced to leave Banduff, despite living in a house from which Protestant residents had felt obliged to flee.

These disadvantages may seem greater to the outside observer than to people who live in the heartlands. For the latter, they may be a reasonable price for an immediate reduction in the level of violence on their own doorstep and in their own estate. It is at least plausible that greater segregation has reduced the level of violence and made people feel more secure. More speculative is the concern that, while reducing the number of local incidents, polarisation has actually facilitated more serious confrontation in the future, by ensuring that the protagonists will be more numerous, more homogeneous and more determined. The dangerous combination of high segregation and territorial proximity had been remarked by Ardrey:

Territory is not the cause of war. It is the cause of war only in the sense that it takes two to make an argument. What territory promises is the high probability that, if intrusion takes place, war will follow.   (Ardrey 1967, 244)

In communities which are becoming more polarised it is often the marginal people who suffer most. These are the people who live in two worlds but are not quite at home in either — they may have married across the religious divide, or have removed themselves by choice from their own ethnic community for ideological reasons. The poet John Hewitt, an Ulster Protestant liberal, was one: 'It long has been my bitter luck to be caught in the cross-fire of their false campaign.'

The person who has not fully accepted the values of the group will be regarded with growing distrust as conflict intensifies, for the renegade threatens not only group unity and interests, but the values which hold the group together. As Coser has pointed out, the more exclusive the group, the greater is the threat to it from the heretic, as opposed to the renegade. The renegade is easily classified with the enemy and attracts the straightforward hatred reserved for traitors. The heretic, on the other hand, is more dangerous because he maintains the group's basic values and remains associated with it, while challenging some of its actions and stances. He therefore has the effect of blurring the boundary between the conflicting groups at a time when the dynamics of conflict are stressing the importance of maintaining them. As Shibutani and Kwan expressed it in 1971: 'Anyone who points out that his own side is not faultless is seen as a traitor and is sometimes ostracised.'

The marginal man suffers the disadvantage of being regarded as either heretic or renegade, depending on the stage which the conflict has reached. He suffers the further disadvantage of being so regarded by both groups in the conflict. The danger of moving away from one's own community was well summarised by one of the best-known examples, Gerry Fitt:

> If you leave one tribe in Northern Ireland, you're lambasted for being a traitor and having sold out, but the other side will view you with suspicion. It is very cold out there if you are de-tribalised.   (*Observer*, 20 December 1981)

Kuper has shown how the middle ground was a major target for attack during the Algerian war (Kuper 1977, 115). There were few such attacks, however, in either Kileen/Banduff or the North Ashbourne estates, because the marginal ground was so sparsely populated. The small number of mixed-marriage families had either left the area or opted for membership of one or other community. Middle class families, which often predominate among marginal people, were also rare. The people who attempted to maintain cross-religious contacts in Banduff attracted little interest during a period when both sides feared the other. There is little room in the heartlands for marginal people, and few of them are attracted to live there.

10.

The Controls on Conflict

A STRONG underlying theme in the analysis of social conflict is its tendency towards unqualified violence between the participants. 'To introduce the principle of moderation into the theory of war itself,' Clauswitz wrote in relation to international conflicts, 'would always lead to logical absurdity.' In internal conflicts too, according to Coleman, 'the harmful and dangerous elements drive out those which keep the conflict within bounds'; he described this as a 'Gresham's law of conflict' (Coleman 1957). Even Simmel, the apostle of sociality, believed that 'every war in which the belligerents do not impose some restriction on the use of possible means...becomes a war of extermination' (Lawrence 1976, 140). A major element in this process, at both international and community levels, is a growing willingness to view one's opponents as a distinct and malevolent species against which the most extreme measures are justified. Geographical segregation and a low level of contact between the antagonists greatly enhance this view.

So the duration of a conflict and increased levels of segregation are often important factors in intensifying inter-group hatred and violence. Both conditions appear to apply in Northern Ireland, and particularly in those communities which have suffered from intimidation. In some respects it could be claimed that the conflict between Catholic and Protestant has gone on for more than three centuries; its latest period of prolonged violence endured from 1969 to 1986, longer than ever before. During these years the levels of segregation and political polarisation have certainly increased in the intimidated districts, and probably in general. Nevertheless there is strong evidence that community violence has diminished rather than risen in intensity at both provincial and local levels.

Having reached a peak of 468 deaths in 1972, there was a decline
in the annual casualty figures to sixty-four in 1984; the proportion of civilian — as opposed to admitted combatant — deaths
diminished, and deaths from direct violence between the communities almost disappeared. By 1984 it was difficult to find
any examples of the sectarian rioting which had been the main
form of violence in 1969 and 1970. It was as if the conflict had
reached a peak around 1972, like 'the wall' in a marathon race,
and subsequently settled down to 'an acceptable level of
violence'. The question is: why did it develop in this way rather
than drawing the two communities into more violent confrontation?

One reason is to be found in the dynamic of the violence itself.
Since 1970 its main form has changed from sectarian rioting into
a guerrilla war between republican paramilitaries and the
British army. From then the conflict was increasingly fought
through surrogates, and became somewhat ritualised. This
allowed many people from both sides to withdraw from direct
involvement in violence, supporting but not participating
directly in the battle between their champions. In addition, at
least one major cause of mass rioting during the early 1970s in
Belfast — the attempt to remove strangers from one's
community — had been resolved in many parts of the city by the
mid-1970s; it is an irony that 'successful' intimidation in 1971,
by reducing the number of minority families — and hence the
occasions for tension — in urban communities, helped to
account for its virtual disappearance by 1975. However, these
are superstructural reasons for the decline in violence. The
fundamental causes lie within the communities.

Shibutani and Kwan believed that the most important factors
in determining the course of each conflict were the peculiar
interrelations between the combatants: 'What each side does is a
response to the actual or anticipated moves of its opponents;
thus the course of events is built up by social interaction'
(Shibutani and Kwan 1965, 135). This process often intensifies
the conflict by creating a spiral towards unrestrained violence.
In Northern Ireland, however, the same reciprocal process has
controlled rather than stimulated the spread of violence. The
long duration of the conflict between Catholics and Protestants
over three centuries has led to the evolution of social

mechanisms to regulate and control their relationships. These
were the consequence of two hostile groups inhabiting what
A. T. Q. Stewart called the same 'narrow ground'; unable to
remove each other and unwilling to assimilate, they gradually
evolved forms of relationships which regulated rather than
resolved their antagonisms. The mechanisms were each appropriate to particular settings, varying between urban and rural
conditions, and in accordance with the religious ratio peculiar
to each locality. They were not always successful.

These mechanisms have been an effective control on the
spread of violence, and the most significant of them are
avoidance, selective contact and functional integration.

Avoidance

In some parts of Northern Ireland like the Upper Ashbourne,
Catholics and Protestants have effectively avoided conflict by
avoiding each other. 'We were never taught to hate Protestants,'
wrote Eamonn McCann about his childhood in Derry. 'Rather
we were taught that it was for the best that we did not know
them' (McCann 1974, 21). The desire for physical barriers is
particularly understandable in communities which have
experienced high levels of violence.

The principal advantage of segregation is the reduction of
inter-community violence. In Kileen/Banduff, for example,
attempts to maintain a mixed community having failed, the two
groups settled for segregation as a means of protection. From
1976 when the two communities had become clearly defined
and separated, the number of disputes between Protestants and
Catholics diminished greatly; at the same time the number of
disputes between groups within each community increased. The
internalisation of conflict was even greater in the Upper
Ashbourne estates, where polarisation was much greater.
Effectively Protestants and Catholics, in two exceptionally tense
communities, had reduced the level of local violence by turning
their backs to each other.

Avoidance is a less appropriate response to local violence in
more integrated localities. The relatively high level of
demographic integration in Dunville created greater loyalty to
a common community, and this has been a significant control
on sectarian violence in the town. Within this 'common

community' the two groups were conscious of their separateness. However this was expressed in controlled and formal settings. Annual processions in Dunville regularly led to open conflict, but they generally took place on a limited number of set occasions, which meant that arrangements could be made to limit their effects. Similarly, the virulence and extravagance of sectarian exchanges during council meetings contrasted with the generally good personal relationships between citizens. At times it appears that the hostilities have become ritualised and limited to the letting off of surplus steam under conditions which were highly conventional.

Selective contact

Complete avoidance between Catholics and Protestants is impossible in most parts of Northern Ireland. Most people may 'mingle with a consciousness of the differences between them' (Beckett and Glasscock 1967, 188), but they do mingle. It is possible for members of the two groups to develop relationships without abandoning their separate basic allegiances. In Ballybeg, for instance, while they were not prepared to attend the film shows in the Catholic church hall, Protestants often drank in the same pubs as Catholics (Harris 1972). Similarly the novelist Robert Harbinson described how, although he shunned and feared Catholics during his childhood in Protestant Sandy Row, it was possible for him to become friendly with a Catholic family while on holidays in another part of the province (Harbinson 1960).

This position of 'co-operation — but only up to a point' is well illustrated in Kileen/Banduff. Since 1976 demographic polarisation has been almost absolute, and contact cautious. Catholics in Kileen were prepared to welcome visiting Protestant old people for meals in their community centre, but not for prayer meetings. Protestants in Banduff shared in the management, teaching and training in Shamrock Youth Training Centre, but the contacts thus made had rarely extended into broader friendships. Even more graphically, co-operation between two local schools, although successful, was stopped short of a point where the closeness would be seen as a threat to the existing relationship.

So the sharp divisions of the early 1970s had begun to ease in some areas, but the circumstances in which re-engagement could happen were carefully controlled. This sort of periodic re-integration is not new. There is evidence of a similar process in the nineteenth century, when minority families were removed from the same districts after each bout of intimidation. The conditions in which cross-community relationships may be resumed are not constant; they change as local circumstances become more violent or tranquil.

The advantage of these situational variations, when contact may take place in some respects but not in others, is that they permit changes to evolve at their own speed. Even during periods of tension, it is possible for a Protestant and Catholic who would regard each other with suspicion if seen in the other's district at night to suspend animosities and continue to work on the same work bench during the day. Two people who would be suspicious of each other in one setting may be able to develop a co-operative relationship in another. On the other hand this did not extend to exempting policemen from the penalties of war when they were off-duty — even then they were regarded as 'legitimate targets'. Indeed it could be argued that the IRA decision to attack not only off-duty policemen and soldiers, but also men who had actually left the forces, illustrated the tendency for the controls of conflict to weaken as violence continued. The limits to the relationships were determined by the context, and the context itself varied through time.

Functional integration

While relationships with members of the other group may vary with circumstances, certain groups in any community are more disposed towards co-operation. Kirk, in his study of Lurgan, found that Protestants and Catholics from the middle classes were much more likely to be in contact than those from the working classes through common membership of clubs and societies (Kirk 1967). Harold Jackson went further:

> Let us be quite clear, the problem is one of the working class. There have been no riots in the prosperous areas of... the Malone Road in Belfast.   (Jackson 1971)

The business and professional contacts in Dunville also suggest that the middle classes were more likely to support co-operation. They also suggest the causes. Not only are they more likely to live in religiously integrated districts, but they are more conscious of the threat presented to the business life of the town by civil disorder.

There is also evidence that common material or social interests can overcome sectarian suspicions. The main reasons for cross-religious contact in Kileen/Banduff, for example, were shared interests between teachers and shared concern about unemployment in the Shamrock workshop. The Gingerbread group in Dunville provides another example. It included among its members women whose backgrounds cut across social class and religious divisions, but who had a problem in common. The group continued to flourish despite the strong divisions in the town during the hunger strikes, and despite the fact that it included people who had been intimidated from their homes. In all these cases the motivation was a common interest or concern, and the fact that the resulting relationships included people from both groups was incidental. 'Reconciliation groups', whose objective was to bring together Catholics and Protestants, were much less successful in both Kileen and Dunville. In districts which had experienced sectarian violence, the argument that people should get together because they were hostile towards each other was not persuasive.

All these mechanisms act as restraints on the conduct of the two conflicting communities. Rather than presenting a single model which applies to Northern Ireland as a unit, they demonstrate that intergroup relationships should be regarded as a spectrum. At one end is a highly polarised, potentially violent relationship; at the other a high level of co-operation and inter-action. Different communities throughout Northern Ireland can be found at every point. Individuals too do not take a consistent position within the spectrum; rather their position may vary with the setting or situation in which the cross-group contact takes place. Nor is the spectrum itself static; it has altered through time, and the alterations have accelerated most dramatically in times of community violence.

The main function of the mechanisms is to reduce and manage community violence at local levels. They are more successful in some areas than in others. But the cumulative effect of so great a variety of micro controls also constitutes a macro control. In effect they are obstacles to absolute group cohesion for both communities, and therefore to a more extreme and genocidal form of conflict. The variety of local relationships has produced within both religious groups a gap between the members at the centre and those at the periphery.

At the centre is the person who lives in the heartlands and whose contact with the other religious group is minimal. His political and cultural attitudes are not contaminated by the views or desires of his opponents, because he does not know what they are. He is relatively untouched by either the ties or the fears of his co-religionist who lives among members of the other group. The problem seems uncomplicated and the solution — 'Smash the IRA' or 'Brits out' — simple. All that goes on around him, even the internal disputes, confirms him in the uncompromising purity of his position.

On the periphery is the person who lives in a more-or-less integrated area. He shares cultural connections with the other side which, if they do not amount to a consciousness of sharing what Leyton called 'the one blood', create an obligation of decent behaviour. His friends and workmates are likely to include members of the other religious group. If he belongs to the local minority, he may be aware of his vulnerability if violence should spread to his locality. Consequently his inclinations and apprehensions are both more likely to urge him towards accommodation and compromise. In the view of his co-religionists at the centre he is a trimmer.

The Northern Ireland problem has often been described as a conflict between two communities. In another sense it is a conflict between two different concepts of community. On the one hand most people in Northern Ireland, whether they wish it or not, recognise that they are born into a Catholic or Protestant community which shares beliefs, culture and problems, but not a geographical base. They are also born into a geographical community, a small localised territorial group defined as a unit by its members. Both carry obligations and loyalties.

Both concepts of community might be regarded as magnets which exert pulls on the loyalty of the individual. In less dramatic times the strength of the ethnic magnet is determined by a number of factors, including local religious ratios, previous experience of violence and distance from the ideological heartlands. In times of extreme tension and violence, the attraction of the ethnic magnet becomes more powerful. During the UWC strike in 1974, for example, many Protestants felt the need to testify to their membership of the Protestant community by demonstrating or manning barricades, even at the price of antagonising or frightening their Catholic friends. Seven years later the hunger strikes had a similar effect on many Catholics, and Protestants were alarmed by the number of previously non-political Catholics who attended the funerals of dead hunger strikers. Even districts which took pride in their long history of good community relations were affected by the pull. Ethnic identities, like seeds, could lie inert for decades and still retain their fertility. They are activated, not by the duration of conflict, but by its periodic eruption into spasms of intense violence. In the final analysis, however, the more violent the conflict becomes, the more likely are the outlying members of the group to be pulled towards positions defined by the centre. The controls provide no guarantees.

Bibliography and References

R. Ardrey, *The Territorial Imperative*, Collins 1967

P. Arthur, *The Government and Politics of Northern Ireland*, Longman 1980

E. Aunger, *In Search of Political Stability: a comparative study of New Brunswick and Northern Ireland*, McGill-Queens Press 1981

D. Barritt and C. Carter, *The Northern Ireland Problem*, OUP 1962

J. Barrow, *Tour Round Ireland*, John Murray 1836

A. Beals, *Culture in Process*, Holt Rinehart and Winston 1967

J. C. Beckett, *A Short History of Ireland*, London 1952

J. C. Beckett, *The Making of Modern Ireland*, Faber 1966

J. C. Beckett and R. Glasscock (eds), *Belfast: the Origin and Growth of an Industrial City*, BBC 1967

J. C. Beckett et al., *The Ulster Debate*, Bodley Head 1972

Belfast Riots Inquiries, *British Parliamentary Papers*, XXXVI, 1857; XXVIII, 1865; XVIII, 1887

D. Bell, 'Ethnicity and Social Change', in N. Glazer and P. Moynihan, (op. cit.) 1975

J. Bernard, 'The Conceptualisation of Intergroup Relations with Special Reference to Conflict', in G. Marx (op. cit.) 1971

B. Berry and H. Tischler, *Race and Ethnic Relations*, Houghton Mifflin 1978

D. Birrell, 'Relative Deprivation as a Factor in Conflict in Northern Ireland', *Sociological Review*, 20, 3, 1972

R. Black, *The Growth and Role of the Whiterock Tenants' Association*, Internal paper, Northern Ireland Community Relations Commission 1971

F. W. Boal, 'Close together and far apart', *Community Forum*, 4, 3, 1972

F. W. Boal, P. Doherty and D. Pringle, *The Spatial Distribution of some Social Problems in the Belfast Urban Area*, Northern Ireland Community Relations Commission 1974

F. W. Boal and J. Douglas (eds), *Integration and Division*, Academic Press 1982

K. Boehringer, 'Discrimination: Jobs', *Fortnight*, 14 May 1971

A. Boserup, 'Contradictions and Struggles in Northern Ireland', *Socialist Register*, 1972

A. Boyd, *Holy War in Belfast*, Anvil 1969

R. Buchanan, 'The Planter and the Gael', in F. W. Boal and J. Douglas (op. cit.) 1982

I. Budge and C. O'Leary, *Belfast: Approach to Crisis*, Macmillan 1973

F. Burton, *The Politics of Legitimacy: Struggles in a Belfast Community*, Routledge and Kegan Paul 1978

S. Buschschluter, 'ETA froth on top of Basque ferment', *Guardian*, 20 February 1984

E. Cairns, 'Socialisation in children', in Harbison and Harbison (op. cit.) 1980

Cameron report: *Disturbances in Northern Ireland*, HMSO Belfast Cmd 532, 1969

B. D. Clark and M. B. Gleave, *Social Patterns in Cities*, London 1973

J. Coleman, 'The Dynamics of Conflict' (1957), in G. Marx (op. cit.) 1971

Commissioner for Complaints, *Annual reports*, Belfast

P. A. Compton, *Northern Ireland: a Census Atlas*, Gill and Macmillan 1978

P. A. Compton and F. W. Boal, 'Aspects of the intercommunity population balance in Northern Ireland', *Economic and Social Review*, 1, 4, 1970

L. Coser, *The Functions of Social Conflict*, Routledge and Kegan Paul 1956

L. Coser, *Georg Simmel*, Prentice Hall 1965

L. Coser, 'Some sociological aspects of conflict', in G. Marx (op. cit.) 1971

E. S. Cowan, *The development of a rural newspaper*, Dissertation, Department of Communication Studies, University of Ulster 1984

R. S. Cunningham, *St Columba's Church: Historical sketch*, Castle Press, Belfast 1978

R. Dahrendorf, 'Integration and values versus coercion and interests', in G. Marx (op. cit.) 1971

J. Darby and G. Morris, *Intimidation in housing*, Northern Ireland Community Relations Commission, Belfast 1974

J. Darby, *Conflict in Northern Ireland*, Gill and Macmillan 1976

J. Darby, D. Murray, D. Batts, S. Dunn, S. Farren and J. Harris, *Schools Apart?*, NUU Coleraine 1977

J. Darby (ed.), *Northern Ireland: The Background to the Conflict*, Appletree 1983

L. de Paor, *Divided Ulster*, Penguin 1970

M. Deutsch, 'Conflicts: productive and destructive', *Journal of Social Issues*, XXV, 1, 1969

H. Donnan and G. McFarlane, 'Informal social organisation', in J. Darby (op. cit) 1983

S. Dunn, J. Darby and K. Mullan, *Schools Together?*, Centre for the Study of Conflict, University of Ulster, Coleraine 1985

E. A. Eager, *A Guide to Irish Bibliographical Material*, Methuen 1973

M. Esman (ed), *Ethnic Conflict in the Western World*, Cornell University Press 1977

Field Regiment, British army, *Community Relations Report*, 2 July 1972

N. Gist and A. Dworkin, *The Blending of Races*, Wiley 1972

N. Glazer and P. Moynihan (eds), *Ethnicity*, Harvard University Press 1975

R. Harbinson, *No Surrender*, Faber and Faber 1960

J. and J. Harbison (eds), *A Society under Stress*, Open Books 1980

E. Hardman, 'Intimidation' in Seligman (op. cit.) 1937

R. Harris, *Prejudice and Tolerance in Ulster*, Manchester University Press 1972

S. Heaney, *North*, Faber and Faber 1975

A. C. Hepburn, 'Catholics in the north of Ireland, 1850-1921: the urbanisation of a minority', in Hepburn (op. cit.) 1978

A. C. Hepburn (ed.), *Minorities in History*, Edward Arnold 1978

K. Heskin, *Northern Ireland: A Psychological Analysis*, Gill and Macmillan 1980

M. W. Heslinga, *The Irish border as a cultural divide*, Van Gorum, Assen 1962

J. Hewitt, '*The colony*', (reprinted in *Community Forum*, 4, 1, 1974), 1950

J. Hickey, *Religion and the Northern Ireland Problem*, Gill and Macmillan 1984

Independent Television Authority (ITA), *Religion in Great Britain and Northern Ireland*, ITA 1970

H. Isaacs, 'Basic group identity: the idols of the tribe' in Glazer and Moynihan (op. cit.) 1975

H. Jackson, *The two Irelands: a dual study in inter-group tensions*, Minority Rights Group, London 1971

R. Jenkins and P. Smoker, *Northern Ireland: a case study in polarisation*, Peace Research Centre, London 1971

R. Jenkins, *Hightown rules: Growing up in a Belfast housing estate*, National Youth Bureau 1982

R. Jenkins, *Lads, Citizens and Ordinary Kids*, Routledge and Kegan Paul 1983

S. Jenvey, 'Sons and haters', *New Society*, 20 July 1972

E. Jones, *A Social Geography of Belfast*, Oxford University Press 1960

M. Keenan, *Moyard: the Case for Demolition*, Moyard Housing Action Committee, Belfast 1982

T. Kirk, *The Religious Distribution in Lurgan*, M. A., Queen's University Belfast 1967

L. Kuper, 'Theories of revolution and race relations', in J. Stone, (op. cit.) 1977

L. Kuper, *The pity of it all*, University of Minnesota Press 1977

L. Kuper, *Genocide*, Penguin 1981

R. La Piere, *Sociology*, McGraw-Hill 1946

P. Lawrence, *Georg Simmel*, Nelson 1976

E. Leyton, 'Spheres of influence in Aughnaboy', *American Anthropologist*, 72, 1970

E. Leyton, *The one blood: Kinship and class in an Irish village*, Social and Economic Studies, Memorial University Newfoundland 1975

S. Lieberson, 'A societal theory of race and ethnic relations', in G. Marx (op. cit.) 1971

Londonderry Riot Reports, 1869 and 1884

G. Lundberg, *The Foundation of Sociology*, Macmillan (NY) 1939

F. S. L. Lyons, *Ireland Since the Famine*, Weidenfeld and Nicholson 1971

F. S. L. Lyons, *Culture and Anarchy in Ireland 1890-1939*, Clarendon Press 1976

E. McCann, *War in an Irish Town*, Penguin 1974

J. L. Mc Cracken, in F. McManus (op. cit.) 1967

E. McEldowney, 'The Vere Foster affair', *Irish Times*, 17-18 June 1972

N. Mansergh, *The Government of Northern Ireland*, Allen and Unwin 1936

F. McManus (ed.), *The Years of the Great Test*, Mercier 1967

G. Marx (ed.), *Racial Conflict*, Little Brown 1971

A. Megahey, *The Irish Protestant churches and social and political issues 1870-1914*, Ph.D. thesis, Queen's University Belfast 1969

G. Mitchell, *A Dictionary of Sociology*, Routledge and Kegan Paul 1968

M. Moneypenny, *The Two Irish Nations*, London 1912

Moyard social survey, described in Sirockin and Keenan (op. cit.) 1982

J. Mullan, 'Christmas crime control in Andersonstown', *Fortnight*, Belfast, 21 January 1985

K. Mullan, *Research draft on Cookstown*, unpublished, 1984

D. Murray, 'Schools and conflict', in J. Darby (op. cit.) 1983

R. Murray and R. Osbourne, 'Segregation on Horn Drive — a cautionary tale', *New Society*, 21 April 1977

S. Nelson, *Ulster's Uncertain Defenders*, Appletree 1984

Northern Ireland Community Relations Commission, *Flight*, NICRC, 1971

Northern Ireland Housing Executive, *Annual Reports*, NIHE, 1970-84

Northern Ireland Housing Executive, *Moyard Estate*, Internal paper, NIHE, n.d.

Northern Ireland Housing Executive, *Highfield estate*, Internal paper, NIHE, 1973

Northern Ireland Housing Executive, *Suffolk estate Belfast*, Internal paper, NIHE, 1983

Northern Ireland Housing Executive, *Housing plan for Cookstown*, NIHE, 1984

E. F. O'Donnell, *Northern Irish Stereotypes*, College of Industrial Relations Dublin 1977

R. Osborne, 'Fair employment in Cookstown? A note on anti-discriminatory policy in Northern Ireland', *Journal of Social Policy*, 11, 4, 1982

R. Park, *Race and Culture*, Free Press of Glencoe 1949

J. Peel, 'Ethnicity in Nigeria', paper read at New University of Ulster, November 1980

M. Poole, *Evidence submitted to the Cameron tribunal*, typescript, 1969

M. Poole, 'Riot displacement in 1969', *Fortnight*, August 1971

M. Poole and F. W. Boal, in B. D. Clark and M. B. Gleave (op. cit.) 1973

E. Raab and S. Lipset, 'The prejudiced society', in G. Marx (op. cit.) 1971

B. Rolston *et al.*, *A social science bibliography of Northern Ireland 1945-83*, Queen's University Belfast, 1983

D. Rea (ed.), *Political co-operation in divided societies*, Gill and Macmillan 1982

J. Rex, 'Conflict', in G. Mitchell (op. cit.) 1968

R. Rose, *Governing without consensus*, Faber 1971

R. Rose, *Northern Ireland: A time for change*, Macmillan 1976

J. Russell, 'No solution in North', *Irish Times*, 14 April 1980

R. Schermerhorn, *These our people*, Heath 1946

R. Seligman (ed.), *Encyclopedia of the Social Sciences*, London 1937

T. Shibutani and K. Kwan, 'Changes in life conditions conducive to interracial conflict' (1965), reprinted in G. Marx (op. cit.) 1971

G. Sills (ed.), *Encyclopedia of the Social Sciences*, London 1968

G. Sirockin and M. Keenan, 'Moyard — the tenants are angry', *Science for People*, 53, 1982

S. Starling, *The sociology of voluntary organisations in Belfast*, Geography department, Queen's University Belfast 1971

J. Stephen, 'On the suppression of boycotting', *The nineteenth century*, cxviii, 1886

A. T. Q. Stewart, *The Narrow Ground: Aspects of Ulster*, Faber and Faber 1977

J. Stone (ed.) *Race, Ethnicity and Social Change*, Duxbury Press 1977

D. Timms, *The Urban Mosaic*, London 1971

P. Townshend, *Political Violence in Ireland*, Oxford 1983

B. White, 'A city divided', *Belfast Telegraph*, 12 October 1979

A. Williamson, *Community integration in a west Belfast housing estate*, Geography department, Queen's University Belfast 1970

L. Wilson and W. Kolb, *Sociological Analysis*, Harcourt Brace 1949

Appendix

Collection and processing of interview data

The main data base for the research was semi-structured interviews carried out in the three communities. Three groups of subjects were interviewed — members of official agencies, local community leaders and people who had left their homes as a result of intimidation. Each will be described in turn.

1. Agencies

There were two main reasons for collecting data from those agencies with which victims of intimidation came into contact: they provided a context for the community studies, and they augmented and acted as a check on the information from the communities themselves. The main agencies from which representatives were interviewed were: the Northern Ireland Housing Executive, both local and central offices; Belfast Housing Aid Society; ex-members of the Public Protection Agency; ex-members of the Central Citizens' Defence Committee; Belfast Corporation Community Services Department, both local and central officials; officials in community centres; officials in community workshops; district council offices; DHSS offices serving the three communities; RUC stations, both central and local; Army GHQ Lisburn; education and library boards in all three areas; six primary and three secondary schools.

The data collected from these agencies varied greatly in extent and detail, including information on agency policy, relationships with the community, statistics on population movements etc., so the interviews were partly semi-structured and informal. Information about particular families which had been intimidated, however, included the following formalised data:

(a) Dates of intimidation and eviction
(b) Type of intimidation and by whom
(c) Information on other intimidation at that time
(d) Family characteristics — ages of children, employment, religion etc.
(e) Role of the agency in dealing with intimidation
(f) Estimates of roles of other agencies
(g) Views about its social and demographic effects.

2. Community leaders

The basic information about how each of the three communities was affected by intimidation was gathered by means of formal and informal interviews with community leaders. Leadership patterns varied between the communities, so the approach could not be completely standardised, but the main community leaders interviewed came from the following groups: tenants' and community groups, most of which had records; clergy from the main churches in all areas, many of whom allowed access to parish records; voluntary community workers; members of voluntary organisations; youth workers; local politicians; local paramilitary leaders; primary and secondary teachers; doctors.

Each was asked for the following information:

(a) An account of how the community had been affected
(b) Their role, and that of other local leaders, during the process
(c) An estimate of total movements in the area and its social composition
(d) Their view of the housing, security and social service agencies
(e) Present relationships in the area
(f) Cross-religious contacts
(g) Factors holding the community together or threatening disruption
(h) Organisations in the area, and their strength.
(i) Present social composition — age, class, employment, religious structure
(j) Records, minutes etc.

3. Intimidated persons

Twenty families from the two Belfast communities had been interviewed about their experiences during the 1972-73 research. These were supplemented by further interviews from the two areas and from Dunville during 1983 and 1984. All these families had evacuated their houses, and some were still in a distressed state during the interviews. The interviews were designed to establish the process of intimidation at individual level, to examine its effects, and to discover people's responses to it. As it was impossible to estimate accurately the precise number and location of intimidated families, no claim is made that they are representative. However there were no major contradictions between the experiences and perceptions in each area, and there was a substantial level of corroborative data.

Once again the interviews were semi-structured, and the following data were collected:

(a) Dates of intimidation and eviction
(b) Type of intimidation and by whom
(c) Family characteristics — ages of children, religion, etc.
(d) Origin and destination addresses
(e) Role of the security agencies in dealing with intimidation
(f) Roles of relief, welfare and housing agencies
(g) Role of local voluntary agencies and local leaders
(h) Problems faced as a result of intimidation
(i) Cross-religious contacts.

Altogether there was a total of 107 formal interviews, excluding more casual exchanges. Of these forty-four were agency interviews, thirty-three were interviews with community leaders, and thirty were interviews with people who had been intimidated; there was considerable overlap between the second and third categories, and ten of the community leaders had also experienced intimidation. The more detailed breakdown was as follows:

Formal Interviews	Agencies	Community Leaders	Intimidated Families	Total
Kileen/Banduff	11	13	8	32
Upper Ashbourne	11	9	11	31
Dunville	7	11	11	29
General	15	0	0	15
Total	44	33	30	107

The time needed to complete an interview varied greatly. Family interviews ranged from fifteen minutes to two hours; when the respondent was under emotional stress the interview was completed as soon as possible and a follow-up interview was sought later. With community leaders and agency representatives, it was common to have more than one interview, and some people were seen six times in what amounted to an extended interview; the time needed for these interviews ranged from about five minutes (where only simple information was needed) to more than five hours.

On no occasion was an interview refused. All interviews were semi-structured. The key questions outlined above were presented in an open-ended manner, to reduce the danger of leading the interviewees, and prompts were used when information was not presented spontaneously. With victims of intimidation this was recorded in note form, and transcribed immediately after the interview. In the case of interviews with community leaders and representatives from the agencies, some key interviews were also tape recorded. In exceptional cases, when it seemed appropriate, there were interviews with groups of people. For example, husband and wife were both present during eight of the interviews with intimidation victims, and there were three interviews with groups of professionals who had expressed a preference for group interviews.

Other primary data

During the course of the research it was possible to collect primary data from other sources. A number of confidential internal reports from the Northern Ireland Housing Executive and the Department of the Environment were made available. Some tenants' and community associations allowed access to their minutes, and parish records from some churches were valuable in examining popular perceptions about the pattern of population movements in Dunville and Belfast.

Also valuable were the ephemeral materials produced by political and community interests during the period of intimidation, and local newspapers were examined. The underground political newspapers are still a relatively untapped source, and were particularly useful to the present study, as they often present a response to events in the community which was unpolished and unfettered by concerns of censorship. They provide a much more detailed account of population changes at ground level than daily newspapers did. These ephemeral materials have been analysed during the periods when each of the three communities were affected by intimidation, and the analysis incorporated into the community studies.

Index

Academic views of conflict, 5-6, 18-19, 20, 24-5, 27
Agencies, and research methodology, 179-80; provision of services, 101, 113; cross-religious contact, 142, 162-3
Algeria, 4, 165
Alliance party, 23, 107
Apprentice Boys of Derry, 11
Anro, 6, 7, 27
Anthropologists, 6, 26
Antrim, 26
Armagh, 60
Army, 36, 43, 58, 63, 71, 72, 78, 107-8, 122-3, 136-7, 157-8, 168; and intimidation, 73-4, 93; and planning, 85
Arzallus, X., 162
Ashbourne, *see* Upper Ashbourne,
Attitudes, 20-22
Aughnaboy, 27
Aunger, 27

Ballybeg, 19, 24, 25, 29, 170
Bands and processions, 15-16, 133-4, 144, 170
Banduff, *see* Kileen-Banduff
Bangor, 20
Barritt, D. and Carter, C., 19, 25
Barrow, J., 10, 11
Beals, A., 152
Belfast, growth, 9-11; intimidation before 1969, 8-18; intimidation since 1969, 58-61; shipyards and docks, 11, 14; corporation, 113, 115, 142
Beckett, J. C., 19
Birrell, D., 23
Black, Samuel, 16
Boal, F. W., 24, 26
Boys' Brigade, 104, 115
British Legion, 61, 135

Bunscoil, 105, 152
Burton, F., 6, 7, 24, 27

Cairns, E., 24-5, 97
Cameron report, 10
'Carson trail', 75
Catholic church, 14, 36, 94, 149; community involvement, 109, 110-11, 120-23, 155-6
Charlewood, Sarah, 13
Churches, 17, 28, 35, 94, 128-30, 141, 151
Church of Ireland, 100, 114, 115, 117, 125, 129
Citizens' Advice Bureau, 66, 100, 117
Clauswitz, 167
Coleman, J., 2, 99, 167
Community, concept of, 74-5, 99-100, 119-20, 137, 145-6, 172-4; groups, 94-5, 103-4, 110-11, 115-17, 120, 148, 163, 182; centres, 101, 103, 104, 110-11, 113, 115-17, 141, 163; selection of, 30-31; leaders consulted, 180
Community Relations Commission, 59, 125
Conflict, dynamics, 1-3; and violence, 1-5; controls on, 91-5, 167-74; conventions, 144
Conspiracy and 'Conspiracy myth', 83-4, 85
Coser, L., 1, 3, 4, 165
Cox, Patrick, 17

Daly, Bishop, 156
Democratic Unionist Party, 75, 79, 132-3, 156
Derry/Londonderry, 10, 11, 15, 18, 20, 23, 27, 60
Derry Journal, 149
Devlin, B., 149
Devlin, P., 64

Donnan, H. and McFarlane, G., 26, 140
Donohue, Betty, 13, 15
Down, 24, 125
Dowse, Commissioner, 16
Dungannon, 91, 138
Dunville, selection of, 30-31; origins and
development, 43-50; housing, 44-5;
employment, 45-9, 48-9; amenities, 45,
50, 128-30, 134, 142-3; schools, 47;
intimidation, 49-50, 75-81; effects of
violence, 126-38; Protestant-Catholic
relations, 127-36, 144-5; Council
disputes, 48-9, 132-3, 143-4

Education, teachers' attitudes, 22;
segregation 23, 25, 128, 130-32, 149-50;
in Kileen-Banduff, 34-5, 67, 101; in
Upper Ashbourne, 37, 118-19, 120,
124-7; in Dunville, 47, 129, 130-32, 147;
see Stanley school

Fair Employment Agency, 48
Fermanagh, 136
Friendship (cross-religious), 100, 112,
127-8, 134-41, 147

Gaelic Athletic Association (GAA), 106,
134
Gemeinschaft, 6
Ghandi, M., 4
Ghetto, 37-8, 148-66; attractions of, 149-
50, 163-4; West Belfast, 66-7, 74-5
Girl Guides, 104, 115
Glasgow Rangers, 115
Grant, Ellen, 13
'Gresham's law' of conflict, 3, 167

Hanna, Hugh, 15
Harbinson, R., 20, 149-50, 170
Hardman, E., 50-52
Harris, R., 19, 24, 25, 28, 29, 97, 135, 140,
170
H-blocks campaign, 60, 74, 75, 131
Heaney, S., 158
Heretics (and renegades), 165
Heskin, K., 22
Heslinga, M. W., 6
Hewitt, J., 20-21, 165
Home Rule, 11, 17
Hoods, 90, 107, 159-60
Hunger strikes, 60, 74, 75, 131

Informers, 159-60

Intimidation, historical background, 8-
18, 58-61; definition, 51-7, 164; in
workplaces, 14, 52-3; from houses, 13-
17, 53; in Kileen-Banduff, 61-8; in
Upper Ashbourne, 68-75; in Dunville,
75-81; process, 85-91, 146-7; perceptions of, 82-5; psychological factors,
54, 55; people interviewed, 180-81
Intimidatory culture, 96-8
Invasion and 'Invasion myth', 83-138
Irish language revival, 105, 152-3
Irish National Foresters, 135
Irish National Liberation Army, 161
Irish Republic, 23
Irish Republican Army (IRA), 63, 65, 84,
85, 86, 88, 137, 138, 171, 173; and
intimidation, 95-6; law and order role,
90, 107, 157-62; and community action,
106-7, 156
Irish Republican Socialist Party, 122
Isaacs, H., 151

Jackson, H., 21, 22, 29, 151, 171

Keenan, Francis, 11
Kildaragh, 25
Kileen-Banduff, selection of, 30-1; origins
and development, 32-7
Housing, 33, 102-3; employment, 33-4;
amenities, 35, 100-1, 142-3; schools, 34;
intimidation, 61-8; Protestant-Catholic
relations, 99-102, 145-6; Protestant
Banduff, 102-5; Catholic Kileen, 105-
11
King, M. L., 4
Kinship, 27, 139-41
Kirk, T., 24, 28, 29, 171
Ku Klux Klan, 51
Kuper, L., 165

Lebanon, 4
Leyton, E., 6, 24, 25, 28, 151, 153
Londonderry, *see* Derry/Londonderry
Lurgan, 24, 29, 60, 171

McCann, E., 20, 149, 169
McGeach, R., 16
Mafia, 51
Magistrates, 12, 14
Marginality/Middle ground, 23, 165-6
Methodist church, 36, 100, 103, 125
Mid-Ulster Express, 46-7, 80-81
Mid-Ulster Times, 46

Mixed-marriage families, 36, 50, 128, 166; incidence of, 25; intimidation against, 13, 96, 128
Moneypenny, M., 20
Murphy, Isaac, 16

Nelson, Isaac, 17
Nelson, S., 28
Newspapers, 26-7, 149; consulted, 182-3; Irish language, 152; paramilitary, 111
Northern Ireland Commissioner for Complaints, 48
Northern Ireland Housing Executive, 33, 38, 39, 46, 62, 63, 64, 66, 77, 78, 91, 100, 103, 113, 120, 142, 182; and policy on intimidation, 91-3, 102-3
Northern Ireland Housing Trust, 32, 62
Northern Ireland Community Relations Commission, 59, 125
Northern Ireland Labour Party, 23
'Nostalgia myth', 82-3, 85, 112

O'Connell, D., 15
O'Connell, E. F., 21
Orange Order, 69, 75, 149
Orangeman's day, 10, 11, 14, 20, 70, 133, 149
Organisations, 24, 128; cross-religious, 141-2

Paisley, I., 75
Party songs, 15, 16, 17
Paramilitary organisations, 67-8, 133, 157; and intimidation, 95-6, 147; law and order role, 157-62
Peace People, 115, 156
Police and policing, 12, 16, 133, 137, 157; attitudes towards, 123, 133, 158-62; community relations, 130-31, 136; intimidation, 59, 93
Polarisation, *see* Segregation
Poole, M., 26, 68
Portadown, 60, 78
Pound district, 8, 13, 17
Prejudice, 52, 150
Presbyterian Church, 36, 94, 104, 114, 125, 129
Protestant churches, 28, 94, 114-15, 125-6; denominational distinctions, 28
Protestant and Catholic Encounter (PACE), 100, 109, 131, 136

Renegade, *see* Heretics and renegades

Republican News, 153
Riots, 8, 9, 10, 11-18, 21, 62, 75, 168; Riot Act, 10
Riordan, John, 14
Rose, R., 19, 22, 25, 27, 140
Royal Ulster Constabulary (RUC), *see* Police and policing

St Vincent de Paul society, 109, 121
Sands, Bobby, 104
Sandy Row, 8, 10, 13, 20, 150, 170
Scarman Report, 10
Schools, *see* Education
Scouts, 115
Segration, 23, 24, 148, 152; Origins, 8-9; incidence, 26; in Kileen-Banduff, 32, 36, 99-102, 170-71; in Dunville, 49-50; in Upper Ashbourne, 38-9, 111-14, 145; polarisation, 148, 164-5, 167; strategy, 67, 84-5, 87-9; avoidance, 169-70
Shibutani, T. and Kwan, K., 2, 167
Shopping patterns, 35-6, 41-2, 45, 50, 100, 112-13, 119, 143
Simmel, G., 1, 4, 139, 167
Sinn Fein, 122, 132-3, 153; community action, 107-9, 111, 123, 155-6, 163
Social Democratic and Labour Party (SDLP), 107, 122, 133, 155
Sport, 35, 46, 105, 128-30, 134
Stanley school, 37, 124-27
Starling, S., 135
Stewart, A. T. Q., 168

Telling, 24, 25
Tohill, John, 14
Townshend, P., 9, 51
Tyrone, 17, 24

Ulster, 10, 43; plantation, 8-9
Ulster Defence Association (UDA), 33, 63, 64, 66, 67, 74, 84, 104, 110, 115-16; and evacuations, 65-6, 88, 112; law and order role, 116, 159-60; and intimidation, 95-6; and community action, 104, 156-7
Ulster Defence Regiment (UDR), 132, 137, 157
Ulster Protestant League, 14
Ulster Unionist Party, 132-3, 156
Ulster Voluntary Force (UVF), 33
Ulster Workers' Council (UWC), 60, 61, 174
United Irishmen, 27

Upper Ashbourne, selection of, 30-31; origins and development, 37-43; housing and social conditions, 38-9, 39-43, 120-21, 123; employment, 40; amenities, 41-2; schools, 37; intimidation, 68-75; Protestant-Catholic relations, 111-14, 145; Protestant Everton-Vestry, 114-20; Catholic New Hull-Avoca, 120-4

Vandalism and 'Vandalism myth', 83
Venner, Captain, 14
Vigilante patrols, 61-2, 68-70, 93-4, 107

Workers' Party, 122

Young people, 40-42, 62; *see also* Hoods